# Garage Sale Mania

This book is a father, daughter
and grandmother production.

D0779743

**God is good!**
**All the time!**

# Garage Sale Mania

A 3-Generation Production
Author: Robert J. Morrissette (father)
Illustrator: Grace Franklin (daughter)
Senior Editor: Barbara Odom (grandmother)
ISBN: 978-0-9763549-5-6
Library of Congress Control Number: 2014945485

**Publisher**
Big Blue Skies Publishing LLC
Coeur d'Alene, Idaho, 83835
United States of America
North America, Northern Hemisphere
Planet Earth, The Solor System
Milky Way, Local Group
Local Supercluster
Sector 28 of the Gamma Quadrant, Alpha
Universe

Cover design and all non-drawings by: Robert J. Morrissette
Printed by: CreateSpace, Charleston, SC, USA

# Manufacturing Compliances

Biodegradable

Made of materials that can be recycled

Organic

Free range trees used in making of book

Gluten free

Non-biohazard, no book viruses

Nonradioactive

Dairy free

Not meant for human consumption

Non-microwave safe

Non-dishwasher safe

May contain nuts

Approved by the International Garage Sale Association

## Nutrition Facts

Servings Size – Per  Chapter (25g)
Serving Per Book About 96

▐█████████████████████████████████████▌

Amount Per Serving

Calories 25; Calories from Fat 0

▐█████████████████████████████████████▌

|  | % Daily Value |
| --- | --- |
| Total Fat 0g | 0% |
| Total Fun | 100% |
| Saturated Fun | 100% |
| Trans Fun | 100% |
| Polyunsaturated Fun | 100% |
| Monounsaturated Fun | 100% |
| Cholesterol 0mg | 0% |
| Sodium 0mg | 0% |
| Potassium 0mg | 0% |
| Dichlorodiphenyltrichloroethane  0mg | 0% |
| Total Carbohydrate 24g | 0% |
| Dietary Fiber 24g (We recommend that you read the book rather than eat it) | |
| Soluble Fiber 14g | |
| Insoluble Fiber 10g | |
| Sugars less than 1g | |
| Protein 0g | 0% |

Zero Trans Fats ● Non-Hydrogenated ● Non-PBA ● No Hexane

90% less cholesterol than other books.
Grade AAA
Made in the USA!

## Vitamins and Minerals Information (daily allowance)

| | | |
|---|---|---|
| Vitamin A 0% | Vitamin $B_6$ 0% | Vitamin $B_{12}$ 0% |
| Vitamin C 0% | Vitamin D 0% | Vitamin Z 0% |
| Calcium 0.05% | Irony 10% | Zinc Oxide 0.033% |
| Eenie ??% | Meenie ??% | Miney-mo ??% |
| Chocolate 0.001% | Caffeine NA% | Salsa (optional)% |
| Dilithium Crystals 0% | Kryptonite 0% | Naqahdah 0% |
| Quarks 100% | Antimatter -20% | Enjoyment 100% |

**INGREDIENTS:** WOOD CHIPS, GLUE AND INK (WHILE THERE MIGHT BE AN OCCASSIONAL BUG PART OR TWO, HERE AND THERE, THERE IS NO MORE THAN AN ESTIMATED AMOUNT OF ONE BUG PART PER MILLION PER PAGE.)

The GS General of Scientific Research and Development has determined that weekly readings of this product will promote optimal experience, especially when "consumed" just prior to going garage saling. In addition, exposure of this product to laboratory rats has produced no significant metabolical, biological, psychological, physiological or theological changes or side-effects. That the rats' IQs may have increased as a result is purely coincidental and as yet unconfirmed. Research scientists, spending your hard earned tax money, are researching this further as we speak.

For maximum enjoyment, it is highly recommended to read this book with the light on. In addition, do not read while driving a vehicle or operating heavy equipment. As for the rats, it seemed to make no significant difference in their ability to read whether the light was on or off, nor while operating heavy equipment. The explanation for this is yet to be determined.

## Questions

Be sure to consult any local garage saler concerning any questions you may have. For all other questions, we are sure there is an answer out there somewhere.

## Quotations Qualified

(Quote) All quotes quoted of quoted quotees by quoting quoter in quotations (i.e., "quote, end quote") are quoted for quotational purposes only, unless quoted otherwise. And you can quote us on that! (End Quote.)

---

**Satisfaction Guarantee** - We are committed to providing you with quality products as a part of your on-going garage sale experience.. Although we cannot guarantee the enjoyment and fun you will experience, for that is up to you, we sure hope you enjoy this book. If for any reason you are not completely satisfied with this product, please place this book in a large envelop and mail it promptly to someone else.

---

**Expiration Date:** Yet to be determined. You will know it when it happens.

## General Instructions

Do not attempt to read this book while sleeping. No refrigeration is needed upon opening this book. Best if kept below 218°C (the auto-ignition temperature of paper). This book is not meant to be used as a floatation device. If for any reason you should experience technical difficulty while reading this book, please turn the page.

## Notice of Manufacturing

This book was made of 100% real materials and contains no artificial, non-isotropic or quantum ingredients. This edition was created on a computer using 100% recyclable electrons and produces zero emissions. In the making of this book, matter was neither created nor destroyed, but rather rearranged. In addition, at no time were any animals or imaginary friends harmed while making this book, nor does this book contain any biologically altered or genetically modified ingredients. Accessories sold separately. Batteries not included (though none are needed). No assembly required. Some restrictions may apply. Operators are standing by.

## General Warnings

Upon reading this book, you may find a new or renewed compulsion to going garage saling on a regular basis. This attraction, known as Garage Sale Mania (GSM), is a quite, normal response to being exposed to such information, especially after you begin to apply and put into practice the things you glean from this book. Since you have therefore been forewarned concerning this possible reaction, the author shall not be held responsible for any and all outcomes of your behavior, thoughts or feelings as a result. You are responsible for these yourself.

## Specific Warning

This book becomes wet when wetted.

## Disclaimer

This book is intended to be read, either silently or out-loud. Use of this book other than its designed purpose may result in a range of various outcomes, which the publisher neither condones nor condemns. Furthermore, the publisher cannot guarantee either the success or failure of such attempts by the user. But you, as the user, are not to be discouraged from such actions. Such applications include, but are not limited to, using this book as a door-stop, a chew-toy or fetching device for your pet, or to press flowers, to swat insects, to start campfires, etc.

All data is factual unless otherwise made-up.

## Note to the Reader

The use throughout this book of phases such as "garage saler", "garage saling" and any and all renditions of the phrase "garage sale" thereof, are intentional, and are by no means an error, nor are these phrases there to confuse the reader. To assist you as the reader, there is a glossary at the end of the book of these and other such terms.

If you find the use of such phrases too irritating to your taste, we sincerely apologize, and suggest that you perhaps read a different book.

## Note to Myself

- Be sure to feed the cat.
- Pick up milk on the way home.
- Buy flowers for my wife.
- Take out the trash.
- Call mom.
- Have fun!

## Special Thanks

I would like to give a special thanks to my daughter, Grace, for all her wonderful and creative sketches found throughout this book. And to my mother for all her editing skills. And also to my wife for all her encouragement and input.

Lastly, I would like to give a special thanks to all those people who sold me such wonderful treasures at such incredible deals at many a garage sale. You are what make garage saling so much fun!

May all your garage sales be fruitful.
May all your purchases be bargains.
May all the traffic lights be green.
And may your garage sale days always be sunny!

## A Word From The Author

Being born at an early age, I quickly learned, that of all the books I have written, this is definitely one of them. But even more important, of all the garage sales I have been to, there are more still to come.

## A Word From The Author's Mother

*"Of all the books I have read, this is definitely one of them."*
Author's Mother

And you wonder where all my great ideas come from! By the way, she, too, was born at an early age. And to think that this is just one of many things she and I have in common. Thanks Mom!

## Dedication

This book is dedicated to all those known and unknown, countless individuals, who have made the wonderful experience of garage saling such a great pastime. Because of you and your many efforts, garage saling is what it is today and continues to be. Through such individuals, garage saling has survived throughout history despite times of war, plagues and world changes. And it will continue to do so. It bypasses all cultural norms and social statuses. It is one of the few things that has never been influenced by racism, religious biases and economics issues. When the economy changes, garage saling adjusts just fine. When fads go out and others come in, garage sales remain, seizing the opportunity. There is always something there for someone. Garage sales accommodate all, embrace all ages and are here to stay!

In words of the great unknown garage saler of long ago:
*"Garage saling has its own reward."*

And so it is true. *"So go forth and go garage saling!"*
Garage Sale Gus

## Acknowledgements

I want to acknowledge all the people who exposed me to the wonderful world of garage sales. To my friend, Vicki Freligh, who years ago took me on a wild, fun-filled garage sale day. And I was never the same afterwards.

And to many others as well. While some of these are friends, most have been those nameless people who ventured forth by putting out their garage sale signs, inviting you and me to take look at what they had for sale.

And to Patrick McManus, for his humorous books, which made a definite impression on my writing style. And in addition, he himself said, "I myself am a skilled garage saler." [1]

---

[1] McManus, Patrick; The Night the Bear Ate Goombaw: Garage-Sale Hype

So I say, "Thank you!" to all the above individuals, who helped inspire the writing of this book: Garage Sale Mania!

As a child, I remember garage saling was an incredible experience. It was like a giant treasure hunt. I loved the anticipated thrill of what treasure would I find. Once at a garage sale, there was the curious discovery that made one ask: "What is that?!" Yet wasn't this how the mania first started for many of us? We experienced our first garage sale and from then on we were hooked!

I also want to give a special thanks to my wife, Liz, for all her support and patience concerning the many, wonderful things I would bring home from garage sales. I have since learned that the word "wonderful" has personal meaning for each of us, such as, "That is wonderful dear. But don't you think you already have enough of those?!" Besides, I like to believe that there is something wonderful in everything. You just have to look for it. I have been told that somehow I confuse the word "wonderful" with: "You never know; I might need one of those sometime" or "That might just come in handy someday." Or, how about, "I can always use an extra."

**Preface**

Thank you for taking the time to buy one of my books. Now I can truly say that I have sold over 1,000 copies. Yes, I admit that it was my wife who bought the first 1,000 copies. But at least I am not lying when I say I have sold over 1,000 copies. As rumor would have it, I have been informed that she did it to confiscate as many as she could in order to prevent any embarrassment from coming upon the family due to my association to her. You know, like "So you are the one who's married to that guy, the one who wrote that book!" But I tend to believe that she did it out of the kindness, love and generosity of her heart in order to pass them out to friends and family, and to give away as gifts. She said that she would have bought more but she ran out of money from her garage sale fund.

At any rate, you are now the proud owner of the genuine article, containing timeless revelations gleaned much research and from many a master garage sale goer. This is sure to become a keepsake to pass-on to your children with all its wealth of wisdom, humor and fun. (I'm sure going to have a lot of books to pass on to my kids if I don't get more than this one copy sold.)

On a more serious note . . .

Going to garage sales is a lot of fun. It has become a great tradition, and in many other countries as well. Whenever I travel, I love to go to garage sales or the equivalent in other countries. They are universal and are an integral part of most cultures and everyday life as a human being.

I have friends who look forward to going garage saling every week. And they are so very disappointed whenever they're not able to go. It's even worse when the weather is nice outside but they can't go due to another commitment. And when wintertime comes, especially where it snows, the season can seem so long without a garage sale or two or more to go to. I'll tell you, those people in the southern states don't realize just how lucky they are, being able to go to garage sales almost any time of the year. Another great thing about a garage sale is that you can go by yourself or with a friend. No reservations required - just pure spontaneity and enjoyment.

Every day there is someone who has discovered for the first time the enjoyment of going to garage sales. Also it seems that there is something new to be discovered for those of us who have been going for many years. I hope you have many enjoyable garage sales, and I also hope that you enjoy this book as much as I did writing it.

## Forward

Garage Sale Mania is a humorous, fun-filled book, surrounding the wonderful activity of going to garage sales. For consistency and simplicity purposes, the phrase "garage sale" is used throughout the book to refer to any similar activity such as yard sale, moving sale, etc.

## Backwards

Garage Sale Mania is a humorous, fun-filled book, surrounding the wonderful activity of going to garage sales. For consistency and simplicity purposes, the phrase "garage sale" is used throughout the book to refer to any similar activity such as yard sale, moving sale, etc.

## Reverse-words

.cte ,elas gnivom ,elas dray sa hcus ytivitca ralimis yna ot refer
ot koob eht tuohguorht desu si "elas egarag" esarhp eht
,sesoprup yticilpmis dna ycnetsisnoc roF .selas egarag ot gniog
fo ytivitca lufrednow eht gnidnuorrus ,koob dellif-nuf
,suoromuh a si ainaM elaS egaraG

## Upwards

Garage Sale Mania is a humorous, fun-filled book, surrounding the wonderful activity of going to garage sales. For consistency and simplicity purposes, the phrase "garage sale" is used throughout the book to refer to any similar activity such as yard sale, moving sale, etc.

## Four-words

Read Garage Sale Mania!

## Blank Pages

Any pages throughout this book that are left blank are done so intentionally. If it was not meant to be so, they would have been filled all with sorts of words, sentences and/or perhaps images. If for any reason you wish to write, scribble and/or draw on any blank pages, you may do so at your own leisure. Yet keep in mind that doing so constitutes a blank page as being no longer blank. And therefore the publisher of this book cannot be held responsible for that page's lack of "blankness." Such action will amount to a void of blankness of a page.

By the way, this page is not blank.

# Table of Contents

Note to the reader: Due to a case of info-appendicitis (information inflammation), Appendix B has been removed. We apologize for any inconvenience and disappointment this may have caused.

# Introduction

arage sale, yard sale, moving sale, self-storage sale, estate sale, rummage sale, flea market, swap meet, etc., whatever you call it - they all have the same thing in common: the opportunity to find a bargain. That's the big attraction. That's the fun. Whether you are a buyer or a seller, you're a winner.

As a buyer you can always get something at a great price. As a seller, you can get rid of something you do not want anymore. And you make a profit. The wonderful thing about garage sales is that there is always some great new discovery to be made. And the rules are so simple: have fun, make deals, cash only and no returns. That's it. What can be simpler than that!

And why should the dump have all the fun?!

"Why should the dump have all the fun?!" you ask. "What does he mean by that?"

Well, I am here to tell you something of which the general public is not even aware. And it is happening right in your own town.

Now, you thought that the only thing the trash man did was to take your trash and then bury it. And that was it - except for the bill they send you each month. But did you know why they bury it? Do you really think that's all they have in mind?

Some people call me a conspiracy theorist. But they don't know what they are talking about. Conspiracy theorists are always spouting off about frightening things that the government, aliens and others are up to. They use phases like, "Just wait and see" or "I warned you." But what is occurring is neither frightening nor a conspiracy.

Think about it for a minute. Why do squirrels hide nuts? Why do dogs bury bones? The answer is simple. It is because someday they are going to dig them up when they need them.

So it is with the trash company. Because one day, what we called trash will be something others will pay money for. They bury all the trash they collect because they know that someday it will all be worth millions. Yes, it is true. One day when the time is right, they will begin to dig it up. And then they will have the garage sale of the century. Those guys are no dummies. They are making money burying the trash and then someday they will be making money selling it. Who would have ever thought? Just wait and see. (Did I just say that?)

A whole new type of work opportunity will someday emerge. They won't have names like "trash diggers" and "garbage managers". Oh no. They will have more refined, more deserving titles for their foresight. They will have titles like "recycle miners" and "sanitation archaeologists". You would be surprised to discover that there are those in high places who are behind such great business schemes. I would not doubt that such individuals attribute their business savvy to their earlier days of going to garage sales.

What do you think our modern day archaeologists are doing? They are doing this very thing. They are digging up what other people buried long ago. True, they have a more dignified title, for no respectful archaeologist would consider themselves a trash digger. But they are not too far removed from what our trash companies will be doing someday. The major difference is that the trash companies have thought it through; they actually own the land and the rights to whatever is buried in it. In this way, whatever they dig up many years later will be all theirs; they won't be required to give it all to museums to be put on display. And they will be able to sell what they dig up to the highest bidder. But these items won't end up on the black market like many ancient artifacts since it will be a legitimate operation by the trash company.

So my thought is: why throw all that precious stuff away when you can sell it yourself? Since most of us cannot afford the luxury of buying scads of property to bury such no-longer-wanted items. In addition, you will have to sit on it for quite awhile before it becomes time to dig it up. So why not make a profit on some of it now before it ever gets to the dump?!

Now I am no fool.  Yes, I realize that there are those things that are definitely classified as garbage or trash, and they are absolutely worthy of going to the dump.  I think you and I know the difference.  But what I am talking about is garage saling, not garbage selling.

So as I was saying concerning garage sales before I got off track...

You can get involved as much or as little as you like.  If you have a morning open with nothing to do, what better thing to do than go to a garage sale.  Or how about being spontaneous - you are driving along and you see a sign which reads "Garage sale - Today only!" So you pull over and check it out.  Or like some, you can even make it a regular event.

Why not do it as a date?!  You can learn a lot about someone at a garage sale – one's interests, one's buying habits, one's likes and dislikes, etc.  Why, I will bet that many a person has found a future spouse at a garage sale.  And just think of all the money you will save by not having to pay one of those dating services.  What better way to see how compatible you are for one another?  And this way you will know for sure that you have at last one thing in common – garage saling!

You can just hear it years from now, the old couple saying to a young inquirer, "How did we meet, you ask? Well, there I was working a deal with this man over a crosscut saw.  And out of the corner of my eye, there she was, looking over some dishes."

"George, they were pots, not dishes."

"Oh yes, cots."

"No not cots, pots."

"Lots? Why did you go and buy lots when you only needed one?"

"Grrr."

"Well anyways, I knew right then that I had met the woman of my dreams.  I then went home and told my parents, "You will never believe what I got at a garage sale?!" Talk about your garage sale super deal! That would make any garage sale parent proud, pots or no pots.

At a garage sale you get to meet all sorts of people. You get to be outside where there is lots of fresh air. You get some exercise, if you call walking from your car to someone's garage and back exercise. But you would be surprised how much it really adds up after your fifteenth garage sale for the day.

Some people consider the arm motion of fastening and unfastening one's seat belt as being good for strengthening the upper body. So I recommend alternating drivers so you can exercise your other arm when sitting on the passenger side. And just think of all the muscles you exercise while looking for garage sales. The neck must certainly get a great work-out. (I think "Garage-sale-asize" should be the name of my next book! Wow, what a great idea! And I could include a workout DVD on aerobic exercises to do while driving and walking to and from garage sales!)

What started out as a simple informational booklet on the subject of garage sales – what to do when going and how to have one – grew into what you have in your hands, interwoven with humor. Believe it or not, you will find many helpful and beneficial tips contained within this book so that you can get the most out of your garage sale experience. The humor has been added for your enjoyment (and mine as well!).

Last Warning from the Author

Upon indulging your eyes with my eloquent writing, you too may become, like many, addicted to garage sales. You may develop a condition known as "Garage Sale Mania" (GSM). So be forewarned before you proceed any further as you enter into the world of garage sale mania.

# A Brief History of Garage Sales

arage saling has played a key role in the history of mankind. As with all great things in history, they each had their moment in time when they came into being and they continued from there, making an impact on the world around us. This, too, has been true with garage saling. And so I present to you a brief history of garage sales past, present and future.

## Garage Sales of the Past

*"History repeats itself,*
*because no one was listening the first time."*

Unknown

ost likely, the first known garage sale within the history of man did not look too much different than the one's we have today. Though the setting may have been different, the initial concept was there. It probably started with a caveman somewhere.

You can imagine this individual having several old clubs lying around which were no longer of any use to him. Possibly

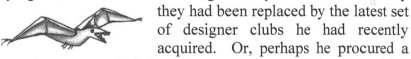

they had been replaced by the latest set of designer clubs he had recently acquired. Or, perhaps he procured a genuine autographed Cro-Magnon Series 1 Club. Just think what one of those babies would be worth today! Probably the only place you would find one would be in a museum or buried in the ground somewhere. If only that cave man knew what one of those would have been worth today! Like most of us, he threw it away considering it trash, only for some lucky archaeologist to find it many years later.

You laugh, but I have learned to have a high respect for archaeologists[2]. You would be surprised how many of them owe their interest in archeology to their earlier days of going to garage sales. Words in our English language such as "finds" and "digs" have their etymological beginnings at garage sales. And where do you think those archaeologists got many of their tools such as old tooth brushes, bowls, shovels, screens, etc.? That's right, at garage sales.

But back to our caveman...

Here's another reason why our fellow caveman no longer had any use for his clubs. It was because spears had become the in-thing. So to keep up with the Neanderthals (that's archaeologist lingo for the "the Joneses"), he went out and acquired a set of his own. And soon he probably just tossed his old clubs in the corner of his cave somewhere as he thought to himself, "You never know, they might come in handy some day." Sound familiar?!

Well, one day our fellow caveman had a visit from a neighboring caveman, who had come over to see his neighbor's new spear. And while visiting, he took notice of the discarded clubs in the corner. As with all great moments in man's history, a thought came into his mind. And in this case, this idea would birth the beginning of the first of many great garage sale moments. (Or, should I say "cave sale"?!) As best as we can surmise, his thought went something like this: "Ahh, oooh moo ugh." Roughly translated means, "Hey, those discarded clubs would be great for firewood!"

So without thinking about concealing his interest from the first caveman, he asked his neighbor if he could have his old clubs for firewood. Which probably went something like this: "Ooo ah ra!" while pointing at the clubs and violently jumping up and down, and throwing dirt into the air. Upon seeing the

---

[2] "An archaeologist is the best husband a woman can have. The older she gets, the more interested he is in her." (Agatha Christie, author & amateur archaeologist, alias garage saler)

neighboring caveman's enthusiasm, the first caveman recognized his neighbor's interest.

Now we need to pause a moment to point out a great garage sale technical flaw. It is called lack of non-pseudo-incognito-intentionaleousness[3]. In other words, the failure to conceal one's true intentions. The mistake of our friend the caveman was not that he asked about the clubs. Rather it was how he asked. In doing so, he revealed the intensity of his interest. Thus, this unfortunately lost him a great deal on the clubs.

By the way, revealing one's enthusiasm or dire interest in something is the fault of many a rookie garage sale goer. Just as used cars are often purchased for too much money for the very same reason, when in fact they could have been bargained for at a much better price. All because of showing too much of one's excitement. (Perhaps it was the caveman's drooling that gave him away.) Over time and through experience, one learns to control one's enthusiasm so as to not reveal one's great interest. If you reveal that you really want something, the seller will have the upper hand. But since this was the first "cave sale" for our fellow caveman, suffice it to say, a vital lesson was learned that day. We need to give our caveman friend some credit especially since this is history in the making.

But back to our story, upon noting the neighboring caveman's interest, the first caveman countermoves by asking what his neighbor would be willing to trade for the discarded clubs.

Again, we pause to take note how he does not go first, by suggesting a price. Instead, he puts the pressure on the other guy. Brilliant move, I must say. Thus, we have the makings of another garage sale counter-play.

As it continues, the neighboring caveman offers him a fur skin, some food, a rock, a T-Rex tooth, etc., in an attempt to bargain with his friend. The first caveman then makes his next move by bragging about all the hunting trips he had gone on where he used the club to single-handedly bring-down a Saber-

---

[3] This is a portmanteau, or otherwise known as a Rob-ism.

tooth tiger. He even points out its remarkable features such as durability, balance and grain pattern. He also demonstrates its versatility, which it can be used for both right and left handed homo-sapiens. (Aren't thumbs great!) As yet, no price has been established.

The neighboring caveman then diplomatically points to the amount of dust on the clubs from disuse saying, "Ugh mum ru nog", which roughly translates into: "This looks rather old to me. And this other one has a lot of dents in it." This edge enables him to justify bargaining for a lower trade.

As you can imagine, this goes back and forth until they arrive to some sort of an agreement, trading the clubs for fur skins and/or food.

Now perhaps you didn't know it, but money hadn't been invented yet. That came later when man began to realize how inconvenient it was to carry around lots of furs, food and rocks each time one went garage saling. Can you imagine having to carry all that stuff around every time you went garage saling? Yes, we owe it to these cavemen for the invention of garage sales, which in turn led to the creation of money.

And so we have the makings of the first garage sale, or "cave sale." This is where the phrase "One man's old club is another man's firewood" came from. Today, this phrase has evolved to what we now know as "One man's junk is another man's treasure." (Well, at least it makes sense to me.)

Now when you think about it, it seems rather amazing to comprehend that two homo-sapiens would coincidentally conceive two distinct but inseparable revelations of compatible germaneness having such incredible future significance and impact, which entered into their cerebral hemispheres relevant to their time and space dimensions yet pertinent to the environment encompassing them. In layman terms, a miracle took place! The chances that this event did happen are astronomical! If any of these and many more such factors had been off at all in the slightest, all would have been lost and the creation of the garage sales may never have occurred. We owe much to these fine cavemen. Yet, we do indeed know that this event took place because of the mere fact that garage sales exist today. This testifies to this great moment in history. (Isn't deductive reasoning wonderful?! You can take it to any conclusion you like!)

Please note the picture showing two cavemen. Here we have one of the earliest known records of the garage sale phenomena taking place. This picture is an artist's rendition of early cave drawings. In this etching, we see that one caveman is hitting the other one over the head apparently with a club.

Evidently, anthropologists have been able to deduce some amazing things from pictures like this one. In this picture we have an actual recording of one caveman expressing his economic dissatisfaction with another caveman over their sales transaction. (I am always amazed that one can deduce so much from just one image.) This apparently was how it was done in caveman culture. Simply put, here we have one caveman mad at the other over his "cave sale" purchase.

I am thankful that this cultural expression of dissatisfaction is no longer a part of our culture. Although I must admit, from time to time there do seem to be exceptions. From what I can tell it seems to be especially true of some few individuals. And the only explanation is that such individuals must be direct

descendants of these early cave dwellers, having inherited some sort of "cave-sale" dissatisfaction gene. Therefore, garage saling is perhaps an inherited trait. Wow, I would have made a great anthropologist.

Next we have an early Egyptian artwork, probably from the Protodynaistic period. From this it easy to see that the artist was depicting an Egyptian "garage" sale. (Note the sale sign!)

As you study more closely the history of mankind, you will begin to see that the garage sale phenomenon has always been there. You will see it in every era and culture. It is one of those things that has transcended time. Now why they aren't including this in our high school history classes, I am not sure. But just think how many of us would have loved as a field trip to have gone garage saling instead of to a natural history museum?

Of course, the term "garage sale" did not appear as part of our modern day vocabulary until much later. With the invention of the automobile, garages were built to house one's car. As an added bonus, garages became convenient catch-all places for storing all sorts of items.

Garages sales, as I mentioned earlier, most likely started off as cave-sales, then over time became hut-sales, which became cabin sales, and so on. As man's place of dwelling evolved, so did the terminology for garage sales. Some of these earlier terms are still in use today, such as barn sales, tent sales and yard sales.

## Other Great Moments in Garage Sale History

*"Anything that won't sell, I don't want to invent. Its sale is proof of utility, and utility is success."*
Thomas Edison (1847-1931)

There have been many other great moments in man's history that were directly affected by garage sales. Since the time of the first garage sale, people have been bargaining and selling things for centuries. This has caused the rise and fall of nations. Lovers have met and missed each other, like two ships passing in the night. Great thoughts, deeds, even inventions have been wrought as well. You may not have even realized it but entire wars have been fought over purchasing and sales! Some modern day wars still go on right in our nation's own backyard. They are called: bargain wars.

They say that behind every great man is a woman. But did they ever tell you why that woman was able to make that man so great? Well, I am here to tell you why. It is because many a great woman was a great garage sale goer herself. Well, it's true.

Take Thomas Edison for instance. Where do you think he obtained all the, parts to make his wonderful inventions? Often he did not have the time to go out and get the various materials he needed. Edison himself said, "To invent, you need a good imagination and a pile of junk." He was frequently

11

preoccupied with all the work he had to do: light bulbs to invent, phonographs to create. If he was out looking for materials all the time, it would have cut into his inventing work. Where would we be today if his precious time had been taken up with searching for parts and materials?

So, guess who was out getting him his supplies? His wife. (This is the type of information they don't tell you in the history books.) If it were not for her, we might all still be in the dark. (And some women still believe that men are still in the dark.)

And think what a boost to the garage sale industry that just one man made. Go to any garage sale today and inevitably the vast majority of those items are directly the outgrowth of inventors like Thomas Edison. We garage sale goers owe a lot to inventors. They gave us more to choose from, more options and more variety. What a dull world this would have been without inventors. As Johnny Carson once said, "If it weren't for Phil T. Farnsworth, we'd still be eating frozen radio dinners."

Many people do not realize that Albert Einstein's inspiration for the theory of relativity came from when he used to have his own garage sales. While watching people come and go at one of his garage sales, he made an amazing discovery. He observed that the value of an item being sold was relative to the personal, perceived value by each individual person.

In short, each person placed a different value on different items. In other words, there was a direct correlation between the personal value of a perceived item and its determined value which was relative to the intrinsic value of the item in question.

As a matter of course, being the scientific guy that he was, Albert began recording data based upon the relative expressed values by garage sale purchasers, intrinsic to their very assessment, pertaining to each item. After efficiently extrapolating experimental and extraneous exponents, dividing diametric derivatives, ponderously and precariously postulating probable proficiencies and predetermined possibilities, compiling compound correlated coefficients and then, ordering a pizza while he took a break, Albert noticed an astrophysically significant and plausible trend. He was able to derive that the determined value (V) of an item increased relative and in relation to the intrinsic value (I) times the personal value (P) squared. Thusly, he was able to derive the following equation, better known as "The theory of garage sale valutivity", as shown: $V = IP^2$.

Unfortunately, like most great people, Albert found himself distracted by some other scientifically wonderful ideas. And so he never formally published his discovery.

And so, years later while Albert was contemplating the theory of relativity, he remembered his garage sale days and the equation he had derived. Seeing the similarities, he dug through some old files and found his notes on "The theory of garage sale valutivity". He was then able to quickly adapt this equation by substituting other variables, and therefore deriving the equation: $E = MC^2$. These findings he did publish. This explains why most of us are more familiar with the theory of relativity and not the theory of garage sale valutivity. This amazing discovery only goes to demonstrate how even garage saling has made a strong and profound contribution to the field of science.

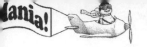

## Garage Sales of the Present

*"A man who carries a cat by its tail, learns something he can learn by no other means."*

Mark Twain (1835-1910)

When it comes to going garage saling, there is nothing like experience. And that is what the present is all about. The best way to learn about garage saling is to just get out there and go. A good place to start is to look is in your local paper or get on the Internet, to see what garage sales are happening in your area.

With the arrival of the Internet, there has been an increased interest and involvement in the garage sale experience. The Internet allows people to post announcements of their garage sales on-line. This allows garage sale goers to conveniently see what garage sales are coming up via their computer and various mobile devices.

But in addition, what the Internet has done, is enable people to sell their unwanted items to individuals they might otherwise have never encountered. It has expanded one's market region. You are no longer limited to the local population of your city. Interested people get to view and consider purchasing items all within the comfort of their own homes.

Awhile back I bought a used cat[4] through the Internet. No, its true. I logged onto the Internet, found a local newspaper's

 website and went to the classified section. And then I looked under section titled: "Used Cats". This particular website had a search feature that allowed me to enter specific parameters about what I was looking for. This helped narrow down my search. Here are a few of the optional search fields: model, age, color, key features and asking price.

---

[4] Footnote:

Upon entering my criteria and hitting the "search" button, up came a whole list of used cats. By the way, I found on another website a used-cat-resale guide. This website provided free information on what is the current fair price for used cats in various conditions. I found this to be very helpful so I could make sure I was getting a good deal. This website also had information on hybrid cats, in case you should happen to come across one.

Using my search results of those cats that fit what I was looking for, I began calling the sellers on my list. After a few phone calls, I found one seller that met my criteria and made arrangements so we could meet. Fortunately, I know a friend who knows cats. So I took him along so he could evaluate my intended purchase.

I highly recommend that you do this too. This way you can be sure that your cat is in good condition and that it will keep running for years to come. My friend was able to check all the fluids and make sure the body was in alignment. He even did a compression check. Although the cat I was considering did not come with any tail lights, I figured I could always install them later. Though the cat had a few minor scratches, it was nothing major. Besides, I could always buff them out. And, as is always recommended, we also took the cat for a spin around the block. Boy, did it purr!

Everything checked out fine. And that day I became the proud owner of a used cat!

Did I say "used cat"? Oh, I meant "used car." This must be an editing error. I will have to talk to my editor about this.

But what if there was such a thing as a used cat search on the Internet? That may not be such a bad idea. So if there was, here are some of the search fields and parameters I would expect to find:

Model: From Abyssinian to Turkish Van, from alley cat
    to moggie[5]
Age: kitten to kitty
Type: male/female, domestic/wild, indoor/outdoor

---

[5] Dog is to mutt and cat is to moggie.

Condition: low mileage, older model, still has teeth, has 7 out of 9 lives left

Features: good mouser, litter box trained, expects you to come on demand, couch-sitter, seasonal shedder, minimum hairball production, speaks multiple feline dialects, purrs in tenor

Misc.: good with kids, does not fetch, low maintenance, recent shots

Options: neutered, declawed, flea dipped, bathed

Extras: If you can get the cat out of the tree, she is yours! Comes with kittens (no extra charge)

Price: set-price, maximum price, "will trade for ...", best offer, free!!!

So with the advent of the Internet, all sort of wonderful opportunities have opened up for us garage salers.

# Garage Sales of the Future

*"The future ain't what it used to be."*

Yogi Berra

The future for garage saling is exciting, which will only ensure its continuation. I predict that someday in the future there will be virtual garage sales. This is how they will work. You, as the person having the garage sale, would purchase a garage-sale-scanner. Just connect it to your computer or mobile device and start scanning your items for sale. As you do this, enter the price for each item. When you are all done, simply submit all your items to a virtual garage sale web site, along with the date and time. All the buyers have to do is download the free garage sale app and check out your site. And now they can view 3-D images of your items. And for those who purchase the garage-sale-virtual glasses, they can view your garage sale as if they were really there. There will be even more features, but I think you get the point.

Gadgets of today will be the items of garage sales tomorrow. And items of tomorrow will be at the garage sales of the future. Take for instance the kid-remote-control. Well, they don't have them now but someday they probably will. And like most new technology when it first comes out, the price will be very high. But think of the bargain you will get when you purchase a used one at a garage sale in the future.

You say you don't know what a kid remote control is? Every parent has been looking forward to this breakthrough in technology. It is a mother's dream come true. When it eventually comes out, people of my generation will be saying, "Boy, I sure could have used one of these gizmos when I had kids." Mothers will be saying, "How did I ever live without one?!" It will be similar to your entertainment player's remote control only it works on your kids. I'm sure they will have an app version of one as well. I'll highlight some of its key features.

First there is the mute button. Just one press of this button and you have peace and quiet. This will definitely come in

17

handy on many occasions. By the way, isn't it amazing how all you have to do is pick-up your phone and at that very moment your kids begin driving you nuts. They start screaming or fighting. Such moments are what call for a mute button.

The next features are the Pause, Rewind and Play buttons. These, too, will be very handy. These will come in handy when there is a squabble between two kids. Most such bickering is over who annoyed who, who started it, or when one is tattling on another. This calls upon you to be the referee, one of your many responsibilities as a parent. When this happens, grab your kid-remote-control, and push the Pause button. This allows you to get your thoughts together and take a brief moment to relax. (Maybe even a nap.)

Now that you can focus your full attention, push the Pause button again, and the drama continues. Being the great parent that you are, you listen fairly and impartially to both sides of the story before making a decision. But now you can do one more thing. Press the Rewind button.

When you press the Rewind button, hold it down until you reach the point where the situation at hand first started. Now press Play. You will be able to review exactly what happened and make an accurate assessment of the situation. Some remote models will include a "Slow" button, which will allow you watch the scene frame by frame. In this way you can see any details you might have missed if you had replayed it at the normal speed. This will certainly teach your children not to lie and they will definitely see you as a fair and impartial parent. And everybody wins!

The "Search" feature will definitely be a time saver. If you need to know where Johnny is, just click this button. The screen on the remote gives you the direction and distance Johnny is from your location. Some of the advanced models will tell you whose house he is at. It may even come with a remote wristband that you can have your child wear. It will allow you to send messages. If your remote comes with a "Timer" feature, this would help by automatically letting your child know when it is time to come home.

The deluxe-kid remote control models will include some special advanced features. Instead of one remote for each child, you can have one remote for all your children. The super deluxe model will be your all-in-one remote. In this way you could control all your remote devices (TV, CD, DVD, stereo, garage door, etc.) and kids with one remote. Hey, maybe there will be a controller for the dog and the cat.

A "Fast Forward" feature would be nice, but it will probably be awhile before scientists figure out how to travel into the future. This feature alone will help prevent many countless disasters such as spilt milk, baseball through the window, flushing the turtle down the toilet, etc.

One of the great things about garage sales of the future is all the nostalgia. Think of all the fond memories that you'll remember when you see some items being sold at a garage sale in the near future. You'll be saying things like, "I used to have one of those!" or "They sure don't make them like they used to." Memories of "when I was a kid" will come flooding back to your mind. Gadgets of today will become tomorrow's instigators of interesting discussion and fascinating dialogue. It is always fun when visitors come over and you can point to some item in your home while telling a story of how you acquired it at a garage sale.

Who knows. I'll bet that this very book you are reading at this moment will someday end-up at a garage sale somewhere. And that's not because it wasn't any good. Some people just don't know the value of something when they see it. Of course

that's not like you. But isn't that the whole idea behind going garage saling?! For example, you might be at a garage sale right at this moment holding this very book. So please be sure to show your support to the person having this garage sale and buy this book. (By the way, I hear that copies signed by the author are worth more. They might even be collectors' items someday.) You'll be amazed when you read this book. (Okay, maybe amused.) And you may even find yourself saying things like, "They used to have garage sales like that?"

As with all futures, there is always the sharing of one's past garage sale experiences with the previous generations. There are some wonderful stories to be told. And what better way to share than telling of your times of going garage saling.

Unfortunately, some us have relatives who for some reason have a story that always has to top ours. You know the line: "Did I ever tell you about the storm of 1932?" And we all know that by saying, "Yes", it doesn't make any difference. They are going to tell us anyway, even though we have heard the story a dozen times before.

It always starts off with "When I was a kid…" and goes on and on with all these amazing facts about when things were harder, bigger and better. Don't get me wrong. I think there is a lot of truth and wisdom in what the previous generation has to say. But every so often, there is that one relative that stretches it a bit too much.

Their story usually starts off something like this: "When I was a kid, we used to go garage saling too. Yes sirree. There was that time back in '32 when I went to a garage sale. Except, we called them barn sales on account of we didn't have a garage. There I was. It was a cold, blustery day with a squall out of the north. There was twelve feet of snow on the ground with snowdrifts twenty feet deep. It was in the dead of winter during a blizzard with gusts up to 120 miles an hour, making it 40 below. (It is amazing how the temperature seems to drop each time the story is told.) We had to walk all the way barefoot[6] and backwards with a double hernia. And it was all uphill, both ways. But did we complain? No sirree, not like the kids today. You kids have it so easy. Of course we had to bring along a canteen, some day old bread and a bed roll in case we had to hole-up somewhere in a makeshift snow shelter, just in case the weather got worse."

It's amazing how the snow was so deep back then. I tend to think that it was because people were so much shorter in those days than they are now. But hey, they were kids back then so everything was bigger and deeper. All humor aside, we do owe much respect to the previous generation--they did have it harder and they sure did appreciate things more.

I never thought I would be doing the "When I was a kid" routine. But sure enough, I caught myself doing it the other day. It must be a sign of getting older. I find myself saying things like. "When I was your age we used to listen to music on records." Upon saying this, my kids would say, "What's a record?!" And they give me this strange look, kind of like what my dog does when I sing off key, turning his head sideways. Take for instance the invention of Velcro™. We find my generation saying to the next generation, "When I was your age, I had to tie my shoes." Or, "To make a phone call, all we had to do is dial; none of these complicated buttons and touch screens." Or how about, "When I was a kid, I had to get out of my chair to turn the TV dial if I wanted to change the channel." Only to hear in reply, "What is a dial dad?"

Ah, but someday, my kids will be doing the same thing. They will be saying to their kids, "When I was a kid, I had to use a remote control in order to change the channel. Boy, did we have things harder when I was a kid. Kids these days sure have it easy..." Things sure do change from generation to generation, but you know, some traditions stay the same, like garage sales and yard decorations.

Just the other day while driving down the street, I saw a house with an old wagon in front of it. You know, the type of

---

[6] Footnote:

wagon that a horse would pull. The owners of the house were using it to decorate their yard as part of their landscaping. Sometimes I have seen people put wagon wheels or an antique hand water pump in their flower gardens. One creative person had a used wheelbarrow in which she had planted flowers.

I've seen several homes with old windmills. One man had converted a horse drawn plow into a mailbox stand. On more than one occasion I've even seen an old headboard and footboard from a bed in their front yard. The owner planted flowers where the mattress would have been. Thus, you have the makings of a "flower bed." One person converted an old boot[7] into a flower pot. These are just a few examples and I'm sure you have seen a few of your own. Here you have some very innovative individuals who have converted old, obsolete items into some creative landscape decor.

I have this neighbor down the street who does this, too. The only thing is, I don't understand why others don't see him as innovative and creative. As a matter of fact, most people ridicule him. He has decorated his yard and so have they. He does not complain about them. They consider his place a dump or trashy looking. But one thing that I have learned about people is that you can't always judge a man on first impressions.

For simplicity, I'll call my neighbor Henry. It seems that every neighborhood has at least one person like Henry. You may even be thinking of someone right now. Or, perhaps you are a Henry. Well, if you are – you aren't alone. And perhaps after reading on, you'll finally feel understood.

If you think about it, these unique neighbors are just being creative. Their idea of yard deco is an old car (or, two, three or more), a couple of 55 gallon drums, roof metal materials, various pieces of lumber, buckets, used appliances, etc. But why is it that you can have a family of gnomes, several bird feeders and some plaster squirrels or even a pink, plastic flamingo in your yard and Henry can't have a washer and drier

---

[7] Bootnote:

in his? If I hang a used tire on a rope from a tree, no one complains. Henry has three more tires than I do, and they just happen to be sitting on the ground but what's the big deal?

Now I know what some of you are thinking. The guy is using his yard as a dump and that he is just lazy and now it has become an eyesore. But this is what most people think who don't have a trained eye. As I got to thinking, this neighbor is really no different than the people with wagons, plows and beds in their front yard. They both are making decorative use of obsolete items. The only difference is that our neighbor, Henry, is just a little ahead of his time. And typically, these Henry-types are very modest, too. For when asked, "What is all this stuff in your yard?", rather than appear all braggadocious, he gives an indirect response. He says something along the lines of he's going to get around to fixing a thing or two, or he has future plans for all of it. Either way, if you really think about it, he's setting the trend for future exterior decorating.

Now think about it, you don't see anyone scoffing about the Jones with their 1890 vintage hay wagon in their front yard. People instead admire it and say things as they pass by like, "Did you see that wagon?!" "What a wagon! I wish I could have one in my front yard." But when people pass by Henry's house with the rusted 1968 VW, people say things like, "What a heap!" or "It looks like a junk yard." What you don't hear is "Wow, is he ahead of his time! He's a real trendsetter." It is sad that people like Henry are often misunderstood and not appreciated. So I want to do my part by bringing more public awareness to such individuals. Someday in the future, you just wait and see, it'll be quite the trend to have an old VW sitting amongst all the daisies in one's front yard. Or even an old gas water heater converted into a lamppost. The take away here is: hang onto those old items. You laugh now, but mark my words, it will happen.

Like all trendsetters before their time, they all endured times of persecution and misunderstanding. People have filed complaints with the city against people like Henry. Some neighborhoods have created rules by which everyone in the

neighborhood must abide, often discriminating against Henry-types. In some cases people like Henry have even been fined. Okay, I agree. There are those who do overdo it. But my taste in art and music and food may line up with yours and so why should it be any different for Henry? You wait and see, like fashion, the trend will change. Someday water fountains and metal milk jugs will be out of style while used tires and bailing wire will be in.

Unfortunately, as with most trendsetters before their time, their ideas were neither accepted nor appreciated until after they were dead. People like Henry are what I call future vogue landscape decorators.

Believe it or not, years ago I had predicted that garage sales would someday be making use of credit cards. Well it is already happening. So the future is already here! All you have to do is sign-up with one of the companies that provide this service, get a credit card reader that goes with your mobile device and you are ready to go. Wow, a lot more convenient than cash.

The whole use of credit cards for all sorts of different types of purchases is great on one hand but it does have its issues. It is great for vending machines for soda and food that take credit cards. Many video games, car washes, parking meters do so as well. I can hear it now. Some machines even talk to you. Some day my kids will be saying, "When I was a kid, we had to use coins to pay for a kiddy ride or buy bubble gum from the candy machine!"

But what troubles me are pay toilets that take credit cards. And yes, they are already here. It is already a bit inconvenient using coins to pay for toilet use. But what about paying via a credit card?! And what troubles me is when they begin to integrate voice automation with this. Don't look so shocked. The machine at the carwash I use talks to me. Some of us already think we hear voices and now the vending machine is talking to me. But can you imagine as they start integrating more and more pay toilets with credit card processing and voice automation?! I can get just hear the pay toilet computer saying, "Sorry, your credit card is overdrawn. You will have to hold it." Or worse yet, "I have some good news and some bad news. The good news is that you have just enough to use the toilet. The bad news is that you don't have enough to pay for toilet paper." In addition, in some places you will be charged per square for the toilet paper.

Like most credit card companies, some will attempt to create an incentive to use their card, such as offering bonus points whenever you use a pay toilet. I don't know about you, but I wouldn't have any use for any two-for-one specials. I only need one toilet. And how about all those extra-value points you have accumulated for all your pay toilet uses. I can hear it now, "You have enough bonus points to get an extra flush."

With all this said about garage saling, past, present and future, it's my hope that you'll show your support in the preservation of this great tradition of garage sales by doing your part in participating in garage sales to come. Have one yourself. Start a tradition of your own, have an annual family or even a neighborhood garage sale. It is up to individuals like you and me to keep this heritage for future generations to come.

# Testimonials

*"A bargain is something you have to find a use for once you
have bought it."*

Benjamin Franklin (1706-1790)

lease take note that while the testimonials contained
within this book are in fact true, the names have been
changed, created or otherwise altered. This was done
in order to preserve the privacy of such individuals from
unwanted publicity and notoriety. If for any reason there is a
story that has any resemblance to someone you may know, this
is purely coincidental.

In addition, many of these individuals don't wish to be
looked upon as being addicted to garage sales, even though
they may actually be so. Later in the book, I address this
growing phenomenon known as Garage Sale Addiction (GSA).
Because of the sensitivity surrounding this issue, many whose
testimonials are presented throughout this book have asked to
remain anonymous.

Now, I call these testimonials, but really, it's just plain old
bragging. Please note, the prices of good deals are always
relevant to the value of the dollar at that time. For instance,
someone reading this book hundreds of years from now will
think that these weren't just great deals, but rather fantastic
deals! But isn't that true for every generation. Each of us
probably knows of a story or two from the "good-ole-days." I
remember my dad saying that when he was a boy, for 25 cents
he and a girl could see a movie, buy popcorn and get a soda
afterwards! (Sorry dad, but I hope this doesn't date you too
much!) He also said that when he went to medical school the
tuition was only $25 a semester! Just you try and top that that
nowadays!

So on with the garage sale testimonials…

- Valuable works of art are often discovered at garage sales, where the values of the pieces are unknown to the seller. One woman paid $1.99 for a painting because she liked the frame, but soon discovered that it was a Rodin original, worth thousands.
- Original glass negatives by Ansel Adams were purchased at a garage sale. The man paid $45 for them and now they are worth millions!
- Another woman almost let a treasure get away. Among the items she was selling at her garage sale was a painting by Jackson Polit. Fortunately someone told her.
- More than once, "official copies" of the original Declaration of Independence have been found. As recently as 2006, another was found, and it's worth equal hundreds of thousands of dollars. In 1820, John Quincy Adams commissioned 200 copies the Declaration of Independence to be made. There are more out there!
- Another man who collected first edition books, had a collection that eventually became worth $20,000-$30,000. Most of his books he bought really cheap. For example, one book he bought for 50 cents and later found out it was worth $250.00.
- A lady once bought an original copy of a newspaper with headlines about the sinking of the Titanic--she later discovered that it was worth thousands of dollars!
- One gentleman found an almost new worm drive skill saw at a third of the cost of a new one.
- How about a new 7' artificial Christmas tree for $25.00
- $20,000 worth of furniture for $1,800.
- I found a free 30-foot telephone pole which I used to make a swing for the kids. And oh, what a swing!
- A family friend found a gravestone at a garage sale which had been missing from the gravesite for 130 years after the family member's death!
- My wife once saw 2 brand new cemetery plots ("never been used") for sale at a garage sale!

- Selling his own toys, a 9-year old boy from Ontario Canada had a yard sale with a lemonade stand in order to buy a gravestone for his father. People donated from all over Canada and even the USA. Not only did he raise the money for the gravestone, whatever was leftover went into an education fund for the boy.
- A man bought a piece of furniture. Upon getting it home, he discovered a hidden drawer which contained hundreds of dollars of cash.
- A solar water heater in perfect condition was once purchased for $10.
- And someday, a mint condition, autographed, first edition copy of "Garage Sale Mania" will be found! Now that's really gonna be worth something!

# Garage Sale Facts and Stats

*"Facts are stubborn things, but statistics are pliable."*
Mark Twain (1835-1910)

or all you statisticians, mathematicians and number crunchers, this chapter is for you! For what research would not be complete without statistical information. If you are not into garage sale facts and stats, you are more than welcome to skip this section. I won't be offended in the least.

**ga·rage** /gə'räZH,-'räj/ (noun) [8]
- from the French *garage*, from verb *garer* "to shelter".
- a building or shed for housing a motor vehicle or vehicles.

**ga·rage sale** /gə'räZH,-'räj  säl/ (noun)
- a sale of used or unwanted household goods, personal items, bric-a-brac, etc., typically held in one's garage or yard.

The term "garage sale" is also known as: attic sale, garbage sale, junk sale, lawn sale, moving sale, patio sale, rummage sale, tag sale, thrift sale or yard sale. Basement sale, patio sale driveway sale and self-storage sale are other terms as well, named after the location of the sale. There is also an everything-must-go sale.

By the way, the term "garage saling" is a real term, as it has been used as early as the 1970s (see graph) [9]. This is despite the fact that it does not occur in most dictionaries, at least at the time when this book was written.

---

[8] http://dictionary.reference.com
[9] Google Books Ngram Viewer: http://books.google.com/ngrams

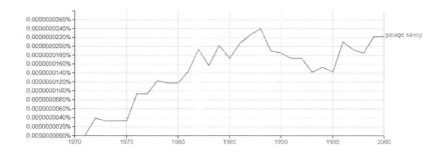

## United States Garage Sale Facts

I have some great news for all you garage sale lovers! We garage salers (GSers) have our very own Garage Sale Day!

### National Garage Sale Day!
It is the 2nd Saturday in August – every year!

Here are some fascinating US garage sale stats for 2013.[10]

| | |
|---|---|
| **Average number of garage sales each week in the US:** | 165,000 |
| **Average number of people who purchase something at a garage sale each week:** | 690,000 |
| **Average number of items sold at garage sales each week:** | 4,967,500 |
| **Overall average price of a garage sale item:** | $0.85 |
| **Total US weekly revenue from garage sales:** | $4,222,375 |
| **Best time to start a garage sale:** | 7 a.m. |
| **Best day to hold a garage sale:** | Saturday |

At the time of the writing of this book, there are 87 US patents that refer to or can be utilized with a garage sale. One of the earliest (Dec 4, 1979) is Patent # 4,176,484 title: Directional Sign. This directional sign is used to point the way to the location of a particular event, such as, but not limited to, a garage sale!

---

[10] Statistic Brain Research Center

The United States is also known for its long garage sales. Not long in hours, but in combined distance covered as a single event! Many of these started out along some of the US Routes (highways) and have grown in length over the years. The following are a few of these.

The Great US 50 Yard Sale[11]
This Coast-to-Coast yard sale runs along Route 50. It is held each year on the weekend before the Memorial Day weekend. 2014 was its fifteenth year.

Annual Historic US 40 Yard Sale[12]

This event has been held since 2004 along Historic US Route 40 from Baltimore to St. Louis, Maryland. US Route 40 was built in 1807, making it over 200 years old. This yard sale extends approximately 824 miles with bargains, antiques, fresh produce, furniture, etc! It is held each year in May or June, depending.

---

[11] www.route50.com
[12] www.oldstorefrontantiques.com

## Highway 127 Corridor Sale[13]

Promoted as "The World's Longest Yard Sale", the Highway 127 Corridor Sale encourages private individuals and professional vendors to conduct simultaneous yard sales.

It was established in 1987 and went from Covington, Kentucky to Chattanooga, Tennessee along Route 127.

Running north to south, it has now grown to over 630 miles in 2014, and is growing still each year. It spans five U.S. States, from Michigan to Alabama. The sale officially starts on the first Thursday in August and goes through to the following Sunday. Hey, perhaps we can get Canada and Mexico to join in!

## Route 11 Yard Crawl[14]

2014 marked the 10th annual Route 11 Yard Crawl. During the second Saturday in August, a 63+ mile stretch of U.S. Route 11 becomes a continuous yard sale that goes from Stephens City, Virginia at the Newtown Commons south to New Market, Virginia.

## Preferred Term Usage

In 2003, a US nationwide linguistics survey[15] was conducted concerning the preferred usage of various words and phrases. One of the questions was:

---

[13] www.127yardsale.com

[14] http://route11crawl.wordpress.com

[15] Harvard Dialect Survey (Vaux, Bert and Scott Golder. 2003. Cambridge, MA: Harvard University Linguistics Department 2003)

Which of these terms do you prefer for a sale of unwanted items on your porch, in your yard, etc.?

Of 10,736 respondents, by far, more than half preferred to use the term "garage sale" over any other term. The term "yard sale" was second, being preferred by about 36%.

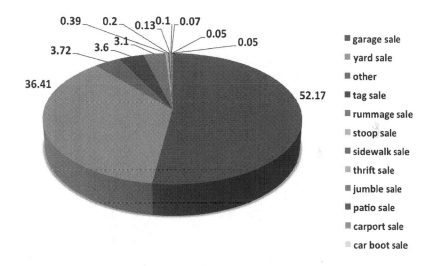

Usage of the Term "Garage Sale" in Books

Upon doing a Google Ngram Viewer[16] search, the term "garage sale" (and renderings of it) has become the most popular phrase as compared to its couterparts. The Google Books Ngram Viewer displays a graph showing how certian phrases have occurred in a corpus of books (e.g., English, British English, and French fiction) over specific years.

Prior to 1974, the term "rummage sale" was by far the most popular. But then the term "garage sale" eclipsed both "rummage sale" and "moving sale".

---

[16] Google Books Ngram Viewer - http://books.google.com/ngrams

Below are the results for English books.

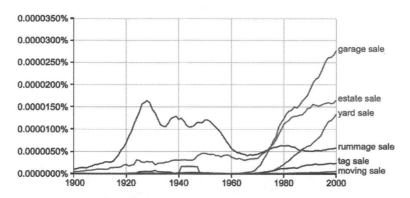

Garage Sale Word Search[17]

Here is a graph of word search activity for the term "garage sales" over time in the United States. Not only has this search become more popular over the years, but it also shows the cyclic trend that garage sales go through each year. In the early spring there is a surge of interest, which peaks around July and then tapers-off through the fall.

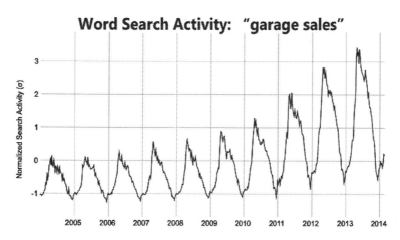

---

[17] Google Books Correlate - http://books.google.com/trends/correlate

Speaking of word search...

For those of you who love word searches, there is one in the back of this book!  And most of the words relate to garage saling!

Garage Sale Populatity[18]

Below is a map of the United States which shows the most popular places for the word search term "garage sales", comparing each state.  The darker the shade, the more popular this word search was for that state.

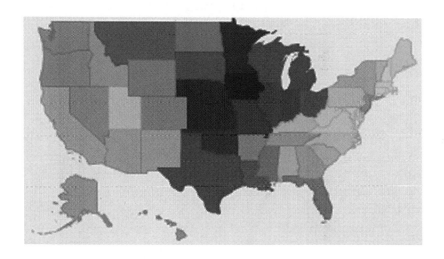

---
[18] Google Books Correlate - http://books.google.com/trends/correlate

## Garage Sales Worldwide
*"The sun never sets on garage sales!"*

Garage Sale Gus

Garage sale euthusiasm is not just confined to the United States. Garage saling is indeed a worldwide phenomenon. Though some countries might use a different term, they enjoy going garage saling just as much as we do!

Almost without exception, if a country does not have garage sales (or its equivalent), it at least has some sort of flea markets. Many countries also have second-hand or recycle shops, such as Germany and Japan. At these places you will find good prices, but there is no haggling allowed.

## Australia

Australia has a national Garage Sale Day, just like us, celebrating Australian's passion for recycling and grabbing a bargain. It is celebrated annually on the last Saturday in October. "Garage Sale Trail" is a government enabled, people empowered, not-for-profit organization that is the promoter for this annual event. This nationwide Ausie event is all about having "simultaneous garage sales that's about making sustainability fun and creative, promoting community connections, stimulating local economies and keeping stuff out of landfill."[19]

## Netherlands

Historically, it appears that the Dutch were the first to have a national garage sale day. Ever since 1890 in the Kingdom of the Netherlands, every year they have been celebrating what they call Koningsdag, King's Day. It is called Queen's Day depending who is the reigning monarch. It is celebrated on April 27, which marks the birth of King Willem-Alexander. If April 27 is a Sunday, they it is celebrated on April 26. On King's Day, the Dutch sell their second-hand items, and do so without a permit and without having to pay taxes!

---

[19] http://getinvolved.garagesaletrail.com.au

## Various Useages of the Term "Garage Sale"

Some countries who have garage sales, or something like it, have their own term for it. The following is only a small sample of such terms used in other countries.

## Great Britian

Called "car boot sales", these are a British form of yard sales in which private individuals come together to sell household and garden goods.

## Mexico

In some regions, they have "tiraderos" (thrown away) in which the community gets involved. A specific street is used and closed off to automobile traffic. Participants set up spaces along the street to sell their wares.

Many counties use the term "garage sale" and/or its equivilent as translated into their own language. The following are some of the terms used by other countries. Keep in mind that these terms are not necessarily used exclusively nor is this a complete list.

| Country | Term |
|---|---|
| Germany | wegen Wohnungsauflösung abzugeben (house clearance sale) |
| Japan | Moving sale or Sayonara sale (good-bye sale) |
| South Afica | garageverkoping (garage sale) verhuisingsverkopings (moving/migration sale) |
| Austria | Verkäufe wegen Umzug (moving sale) |
| Finland | pihakirppis & muuttomyynti (yard sale and moving sale) |
| France | Ventes suite à un déménagement (moving sale) |
| Italy | vendita usato (used sale) |
| Denmark | flytte salg (moivng sale) |

For various translations of the title "Garage Sale Mania", see Exhibit B - Garage Sale Mania Translations.

Who Has Garage Sales

Garage sales are put on by individuals, couples, friends and families. Often neighbors and entire neighborhoods will get together. We have one street that puts on a street-long garage sale every summer. It is common for organizations and even cities get involved. And what Methodist Church would not be complete without one?!

Some groups have garage sales to raise money for good causes. Take for instance the Hawaii Self Storage in Mililani, Hawaii. They hosted their fourth annual garage-sale charity event in September of 2103. All proceeds from the benefit went to the Hawaii Meth Project, a nonprofit organization that implements statewide community-action programs designed to reduce methamphetamine use, particularly among teens.

Even entire cities have joined into putting on garage sales. Here just a few examples:

- The City of Santa Cruz, CA has a citywide garage sale Saturday and Sunday, the second weekend in October.
- The city of Liberty Lake celebrated its 21$^{st}$ annual city yard sale in June of 2014.
- If you happen to be Maine Township, Illinois they have their annual 80-family Community Garage Sale in September. The proceeds benefit the emergency food pantry.
- March 2014 was the 47th annual Garage-A-Rama for Gallatin County Fairgrounds, Montana. And it keeps growing every year.

I bet if you plan it just right, you could do a Garage Sale Tour of the US, where each day you visit a different garage sale in a different city! That would be a family trip to remember.

## Garage Sales and the Environment

One last thing, garage sales are good for the environment. They are definitely a form of recycling. Instead all that stuff going into the landfill, other people are finding great treasures and putting them to good use.

So when you think recycling, think garage sales!

# The "Garage-ological" System

*"If it wiggles, it's biology.*
*If it smells, it's chemistry.*
*If it moves, it's physics.*
*And if it's looking for a bargain, then it's garage-ology."*

Garage Sale Gus

When you take the time to observe the whole garage sale phenomenon, it has its own sociological structure. Or, it is what I call: the garage-ological system. This system lies within a delicate balance. As each part of the system does its part, the whole system continues to thrive and grow. Though it is so much a part of our life, it often goes unnoticed and non-documented. So what I want to attempt here is to present an initial explanation for the garage-ological system as well as to establish a structure of sociological classification.

After much careful observation and analysis, I have determined that all participants in the "garage-ological" system can be classified in one of three categories. These are also known garage sale person types. They are as follows:

o   Garage Sale Generators
o   Garage Sale Gatherers
o   Garage Sale Go-getters

## Garage Sale Generators

Garage sale generators are the start of the garage sale food-chain. Since they are the base of the "garage-ological" pyramid, they are foundational and therefore are the most important. These are the individuals who create all the wonderful stuff that will eventually be sold at garage sales. These include but are not limited to inventors, manufacturers and stores. If it weren't for them, there wouldn't be anything for the buyers to buy at garage sales.

## Garage Sale Gatherers

As the name itself clearly indicates, these are the persons who gather or accumulate the things that eventually end-up at garage sales. Gatherers play a very important role, too. Though their gathering techniques are varied, they generally involve on-going purchases from stores. Sometimes it is thrust upon them by unwanted gifts from others. Sure the garage sale generators produce all the stuff, but someone has to accumulate it so that it will eventually become available at a garage sale. And this is where gatherers come in.

There are basically four types of garage sale gatherers: balanced, passive, active and receptive. Let's face it. We are all gathers of some kind. As you read on, you'll recognize that you fall into one or more of these types.

## Balanced Gatherers

As the name suggests, these are the more balanced of the gatherers. They flow with the system. They are one with the garage-sale-osmos. As soon as new items come into their lives, the old ones are gone. They have little or no accumulation in their lives. One would think they are actually non-participants, but that is not true. Their items go somewhere. It just happens moment by moment. They just don't wait until they accumulate. As result, they never have a garage sale. But they do often donate to others who do.

## Passive Gatherers

As with most people, they tend to be passive gatherers. What typically happens is that they have a natural accumulation of things over time, usually manifesting in their garages, closets, attics or basements. Most passive gathers are initially not even aware that they are accumulating items. Some of the more organized and disciplined hold annual "ungathering" rituals better known as "Spring Cleaning." They may even have an annual garage sale each year.

41

On the other hand, the more unorganized individuals tend to either be too busy or in denial to take notice of the slow accumulation of items in their garage. And then one day it dawns on them. If you find yourself saying, "Where did all this stuff come from?", you probably fall into this category.

## Active Gatherers

As the name implies, the active gatherers are those individuals who are actively gathering items that eventually end-up at a garage sale. There are two types of active gatherers: purposeful and un-purposeful.

Purposeful active gatherers are those who set out to buy things at garage sales that they intend to resell. Un-purposeful active gatherers are those who didn't intend to gather so much but end up doing so anyway. They often are the ones who turn a blind eye to the over-packed garage or basement. Somehow for them, just turning off the light in the garage or shutting the door to the basement makes everything better. In some cases, they are the ones who are actively accumulating items for which no one has any use. It is as if the thrill of buying things at garage sales is what drives them.

## Receptive Gatherers

Receptive gatherers are those individuals who accumulate items by default. As the name implies, they are on the receiving end. Items seem to just come their way, which can be a curse or a blessing. Such occurrences can be through an inheritance. Or, it could be via the well-meaning aunt or uncle who keeps dropping stuff off at your place. They also get things from family members or friends as gifts, or under the guise of "I was thinking of you." When in actuality, the item is not something that they need or would ever want. Sometimes these things are also items of which the recipients have no use, or they already have two or more of the same items. At the same time receptive gathers tend to be passive, unwilling to say anything for fear of upsetting or hurting the giver's feelings. Yet at some point, receptive gathers have had enough, and it all has to go.

So at this point, I would like to introduce one of garage sales' natural laws: the *law of saturation*. This is a very important natural law. It is what helps keep the garage sale phenomena going. Let me explain how it works.

What typically happens is that over time, a gatherer begins storing many unwanted and no longer in use items. These are put in various out-of-the-way places, such as a garage, storage shed, attic, closet, basement, or often a combination thereof. Now over time, one or more of those places will reach a point of full capacity. Various things begin to occur which prompt the person that something needs to be done. This is known as **the point of saturation**.

There are many signs that indicate that one has reached the point of situation. It always better to recognize these signs earlier than later. One such sign is when it has become either difficult, nearly impossible or even dangerous to get through one's garage. Another sign is that the closet door will no longer shut. And if one is able to close the closet door despite the great resistance coming within the closet, this accompanied by a load crunch noise from within the closet. Some even begin to develop what is known as "closet-opening-phobia", the fear of opening closets. Another sign is, that upon opening the shed door, you find yourself quickly shutting the door, deciding it is not worth digging through everything just to get to that one item you are looking for.

These and others are really good indicators that it is time to have a garage sale. The importance of the garage sale law of saturation is that it creates a natural response to get rid of the accumulated stuff. This natural law ensures that garage sale phenomenon continues.

What is unique about each individual is that each person seems to have his or her own personal saturation point. Unfortunately, there are those rare individuals who seem impervious to the law of saturation. All the signs might be there that it is time to have a garage sale but somehow they

seem to resist more than others. Thus the saying, "You can lead a man to his garage but you can't make him have a garage sale." I am not sure how it happened, but somehow this saying evolved from something to do with horses and water.

## Garage Sale Go-getters

As the name implies, these are the people who go and get the stuff that the gatherers have been gathering. These are the attendees of garage sales. What is interesting about these individuals is that with the use of a very simple device, they can be quickly identified. It is as if they are wired to respond, and leap into action almost unconsciously. All it takes is the display of a simple sign with the words "Garage Sale" and with an arrow pointing them in the right direction, and they are off and running. Amazing!

Garage Sale Go-getters can be divided into four different categories. Each of these has its unique traits. These categories are as follows:

## The "Once-in-awhilist"

These individuals rarely attend garage sales. If they do, they mainly do so out of curiosity or just for something to do on a Saturday morning. Or, they could be the neighbor next store who really stopped by to borrow your lawnmower or a cup of sugar, and just happened to do so on the day of your garage sale.

## The Enthusiast

These folks are out to have a good time. They hope to find a good bargain but are content if they don't. They simply enjoy being outside, interacting with others and swapping stories. And going garage saling is just one of many activities that provides a good opportunity to do just that.

## The Hobbyist

Hobbyists are also known as collectors. These are the ones who are very selective about what they are looking for. They are focused, wanting to add one or more items to their  collection or collections. Some examples are antiques, tools, Elvis paraphernalia, lava lamps, buttons or almost anything, but they usually have very specific items in mind. You can always spot Hobbyists. They are the ones who ask questions that start like: "Do you have any ....?"

There are two types of hobbyists: the non-serious and the serious. Most start out as the non-serious type. They have certain items of interest, and from time to time, they add an item or two to their collection. Nothing really serious is going on. But as things continue, many of these individuals transform from non-serious to serious types. It is not quite known at what moment this change takes place. Rather than explain this metamorphosis, I will illustrate.

The other day, my mom met a husband and wife who went from non-serious to serious. It was her friend's acquaintance, once-removed. (I have a cousin that is twice-removed. Yet no matter how many times we've removed him, he kept coming back. But that's family for you. Once you are born into a family, you'll always be a part of it.)

Anyway, this woman and her husband loved to travel. And when they did, they go would garage saling along the way. He collected car license plates and she collected all sorts of items. Now, years later, their house is full of items they have bought at garage sales. It is like an antique museum, and they even give tours! To store and display the many treasures they have acquired, they have dedicated cabinets for this very purpose. They have even purposely added onto their house just so they could have more rooms for all their stuff. At what point they went from non-serious to serious is unknown. But one look at their house and you know you have met a serious hobbyist garage saler!

## The Professional

These individuals know all the tricks of the trade. They know how to bargain, where to look, what's the market and resale value of various items, etc. Many times they buy in bulk. This is when they make any offer to buy several things, instead of paying full price if they had bought those things separately. You can learn a lot from a professional. They are easy to recognize. They are usually the ones who will show up at your door one hour before your garage sale is to start. Or, they show-up at the end offering to buy many of your items at super low prices.

## The Addict

These are those individuals who are hooked on garage sales. They are garage sale addicts (GSA). They can't pass up a garage sale. No matter how tired they might be on any given day, they will perk-up when the words "garage sale" are spoken. They can't wait for the next garage sale. Garage saling seems to be in their blood. It was what they were born to do. Hey, everyone needs a purpose in life, and what better purpose than garage saling!

As for the addict, when it comes to garage saling, the words "need" and "want" seem synonymous. These individuals often become overly angry when anything interferes with their sacred garage sale day, or should I say "days." These are people who can't stay away from a garage sale. There seems to be a rush or natural high they get from going to garage sales. They find it very hard to resist. One isn't enough. There is an inner compulsion that says, "Maybe just one more." If it's not one garage sale, it's the next, then the next. If it's not one weekend, it's the next weekend, then the one after that.

While waiting for the next garage sale, they are talking with fellow addicts about their garage sale exploits. It's as if they have a sixth-sense - able to find other garage sale junkies in a coffee shop. They recruit; they begin to get others involved.

Where I live, we have a snow season. When it gets cold, the garage sale addicts go into hibernation. During the winter, they begin saving, contemplating, planning, and waiting. And then upon the first signs of spring, they come out of the woodwork, because that is when garage sale season begins. On the positive side, garage sale addicts appear, on the outside, to be relatively harmless to society and to themselves.

What is interesting to note is that the number of individuals in this particular category, known as garage sale addicts, seem to be increasing at a much higher rate than we first thought. So I felt it my duty to study this issue and to write about my findings in the next chapter.

# Garage Sale Addicts

*"A man with an obsession is a man who has very little sales resistance."*

C.S. Lewis (1898-1963)

arage sale addicts, better known as GSAs, are among us. As surprising as it might seem, people you may even know may be GSA (not to be confused with Girl Scouts of America). You might be one yourself and may not even realize it. Please do not panic. It is more common than you think. You are not alone. It is my advice that if, for any reason, you think or suspect, or it has been pointed out to you by a respected friend, that you may be showing signs of garage sale addiction, otherwise known as Garage Sale Mania (GSM), you should seek professional help. You should by no means be ashamed of it. If you find that you are a GSA, there is help. Many struggle with GSM. It ranks up there with addiction to chocolate (although some, like myself, consider chocolate a food group unto its own. Chocolate comes from a bean, does it not?!).

You may find this hard to believe, especially since this is probably the first time you have ever heard about GSM. The reason you don't hear anything about it in the news is because most people are happy with their addiction. GSM is a socially accepted behavior. This is despite the fact that a GSA has all the typical signs of a true addiction. Here are just a few of such signs:

Denial: "I'm not addicted to garage sales. I can stop whenever I want. I just don't want to right now."

Justification: "Think of all the money we are saving." Or, "Look at all the bargains."

Pre-occupation: lots of time, energy, weekends and money being consumed with one's addiction. It's definitely not keeping people off the streets.

Language: GSAs have nicknames such as garage sale fanatics, garage sale junkies, etc. They use words and phrases like "stuff", "fix", "hooked" on garage sales and "one is not enough".

It is hard to argue with this type of reasoning. Most GSAs would not even consider it an addiction but rather a hobby, a family tradition, a fun activity or "just something we do." By all outward appearances it seems very harmless. Besides, no one is getting hurt. But that's as it appears on the outside.

Just you wait and see. One of these days you will see one of those talk show about "How garage saling ruined my marriage." You will hear testimonials of "Well I know it wasn't right for me to spend all our life savings at garage sales but I just couldn't stop." I think that the professional community needs to seriously consider this and prepare for it.

One thing I have observed about GSAs is their use of certain words and phrases. As with most addicts, they have their own lingo. And by knowing some of these phrases, it allows you to recognize GSAs in your midst. They use phrases such as "You never know when I might need one of these", "It might come handy one day" or "I'll buy this for so-and-so." You can pick a GSA out of a crowd just by mentioning the word "garage sale." They suddenly come alive and look your way with an expression that says, "Did someone say garage sale?!"

Please be aware that I have spent much of my own time and money attending garage sales, researching the plight of GSA and hoping that it does not become an epidemic. I also hope that the psychiatric profession will begin to give some serious thought to this growing problem. No one in the medical community seems to be taking me seriously.

Therefore, I have decided that I must take matters into my own hands. Any contributions to my research would be accepted with much gratitude. Unfortunately, such contributions are not tax deductible at this time. But be assured that every dollar that you give will be spent at garage sales doing research. In this way, our research team can experience firsthand what it is like to be a GSA--you know,

their thoughts, feelings, impulses, etc. Once the probable cause has been narrowed down, the next phase will involve development of a cure. The goal is help GSAs have a normal garage sale experience without all the disruptions of an addictive life-style.

Being on the cutting edge of GSM research, I have developed a means of determining if a person has GSM. Having four or more of the following traits strongly suggests that you may be struggling with early signs of GSM.

**GSM Score**

Read through each of the following statements. Put a checkmark next to each statement that is true about you. Otherwise, leave it blank.

_____ You find your head rapidly turning either to the left or right upon passing a garage sale sign.

_____ The thought of resisting a garage sale sign is worse than spilling your coffee while braking to view one.

_____ As spring begins, you notice that you become anxious. You have this sudden growing urge to get out of the house, drive around the neighborhood and spend money.

_____ You find yourself turning to the classified section of the newspaper before you look at any other section. (The Internet equivalent is spending hours viewing the classifieds or on web sites that host garages sales or auctions.)

_____ The mere mention of the phrase "garage sale", "bargain" or any of its counterparts immediately causes your heart rate to increase.

_____ When asked, "What would you like to do today?" your first thought is, "Let's go garage-selling!"

_____ You carry change and small bills around for the sole purpose of going garage saling.

_____ You walk very fast or run to garage sales to beat others to the good stuff.

_____ You text or send photos to your friends, showing them all the great stuff you got.

_____ Upon being confronted that one might be addicted to garage sales, your response is, "I'm not addicted. I can quit anytime I want to."

_____ Because of a garage sale, you've been late to appointments or other engagements. Or, you have left such events early or in the middle of them just to go to a garage sale.

_____ You start to recognize other garage sale regulars at garage sales, and suddenly you realize that you have become a regular.

_____ You have run a red light or stop sign while trying to read a garage sale sign.

_____ You plan your day and even your weekend around garage sales. Or, you go garage saling even when on holiday.

_____ When someone dies, your first thought is: "Will there be an estate sale?"

Now count the total number of checkmarks you made. This is your GSM score. Determine your level of GSM using the GSM scale below.

**GSM Scale**

4-6 Low GSM – early signs of GSM.

7-9 Medium GSM – secondary onset of GSM.

10 or more: High GSM – in danger of becoming a GSA!!!

If you have Low GSM, this is not necessarily something to concern yourself with. If you have Medium GSM, you will want to take precautions and begin monitoring yourself. But if you have High GSM, it is strongly recommended that you get help. I encourage you to join a Garage Sale Addicts Anonymous (GSAA) group and also see a therapist.

Some attribute GSM to a genetic disorder. As a matter of fact, you yourself may have come from a long line of GSAs.

Perhaps you are related to our historic garage saler, Mr. Neanderthal (mentioned earlier in this book).

I'm sure that with all the money being spent on genetic research, scientists will be able to give us a more definite answer, and possibly even find a cure. Hopefully, someday they will be able to identify a specific gene that is to blame - that little culprit! Aren't genes wonderful?! They give people something to excuse their behavior so they don't have to be responsible for their actions. I can see it now, people will someday be saying, "You see, I can't help it; it's in my genes." Or, "My genes made me do it." Just try telling that one to your spouse!

I'll bet a whole branch of psychology will emerge someday where they can determine your personality type just by what type of things you typically accumulate. They will most likely take this one step further by factoring in where you typically store your unwanted items: closets, garage, attic or basement. They will cross-reference this to your average garage sale purchase, and then multiply it by your garage sale attendance record. From this they'll be able to derive your garage sale coefficient. What is your garage sale coefficient (GSC)? I have no idea. But you know how those psychologists are. They are always publishing papers and coming up with new terminology to confuse us normal people so they can sound quite amazing. And they also do it so they can get their PhDs.

## PhG

I realized something the other day. As far as I can tell, no college or university offers a degree having to do with garage saling. While you can get a BS in Turf and Golf Course Management, an AS in Bowling Industry Management, or even a BS in Theme Park Engineering and Technology, there's been nothing for us garage salers ... until now!

So here's what I'm going to do for you. I'm going to grant you the ability to obtain your official PhG: **P**articipant of **H**umankind in **G**arage-Sale-ology. That's right! And better yet, no thesis papers or dissertations, requiring lots of big words, citations and references. There's no excessive use of government funding. No fees are required. Just turn to Appendix A in this book. In four easy steps, you will be granted your PhG. And when you do, you too can then say, "I have my PhG!"

## Confessions of a Garage Sale Addict

The following are real confessions from some self-diagnosed GSAs. You may find this helpful as you may be able to relate to their confessions. It is also reassuring to know that you are not alone. While their names have been changed to hide their identity, their confessions are true.

You know you are addicted to garage sales when:

"... I keep thinking, 'Maybe the next one will be the big one! Maybe I'll hit it big.'" – Kelly S.

"... I don't need one earthly thing in the world. But I still go every weekend." – Alley Cat

"... I cannot go a weekend without going to garage sales!" – Alice M.

"... I dream about waking up very early on a Saturday morning to go to every garage sale before anyone else so I get the best stuff!" – Tom Franklin

"... I'm all packed up and on my way out of town, and then I see those bright green or pink signs and I want to stop and pick up a bargain!" – The Happy Garage Saler

"... I have a garage sale and it's all stuff I got at other garage sales." – Jim Shorts

"... I'm on my way to a doctor's appointment and I see a garage sale sign, and I've got a tough decision to make."
– Ima GSA

"... I've plotted out my course the night before, map questing directions and marking the newspaper with order of priority. I've awakened at 3 a.m., disappointed that it was too early to get up and get going." – Mary

"... everywhere you go, you run into the same people. There's a whole network of regulars out there, and you see them every weekend. (and now I'm one of them!)"
– Hooked on Garage Sales

"... every weekend I vow to only go to a couple or none at all, and then the addiction takes over and I spend two days running from house to house in search of - I don't know; I don't care - it's the search and the bargains I can't pass up." – Debbie

"... I left my friend's wedding reception for about an hour to make a quick visit to a garage sale I had seen on the way in. I went back to the reception with my car full of treasures!" – AJ

"... it dawns on you that when gamblers win they are hooked even deeper. It's no different for a garage sale addict." – Pete Moss

Personally, I think the government knows about this garage sale addiction epidemic and they aren't going to do anything about it. They are keeping it a secret from the public. They know that our economy lies in a very delicate balance and that there are certain key factors that keep us from economic disaster. And, garage sales are a very necessary part of this economic equation. So, we need to keep doing our part by having garage sales and going to them as well - while keeping the garage sale mania under complete control, of course!

# Garage Sale Mania Research

*"Our investigations have always contributed more to our amusement than they have to knowledge."*

Will Rogers (1879-1935)

After spending billions of dollars of government funding, scientists have determined that there seems to be a direct correlation between the increase in the number of garage sales and the rise in the average temperature of the outside air. As of now, the research is inconclusive. Further research is being conducted as we speak.

Incidentally, these are the same scientists who did research noting that there is also a direct correlation between the drop of ice cream sales and the time of year when leaves begin falling off trees. This research is inconclusive and on-going as well. (But it keeps those research scientists employed.)

Although scientists have not yet been able to account for this aforementioned phenomenon involving garage sales, do not fear, for I have devised my very own hypotheses. This phenomenon is better known as Garage Sale Mania (GSM). Evidently, certain types of people are more prone to this mania while others have a much higher immunity.

After doing a little research myself, I came up with some interesting statistics. Using the highly reputable "throw-the-dart-at-the-map" method, I randomly picked a city: Seattle, WA. I then gathered the appropriate statistics, ran my calculations and plotted my findings as shown on the following graphs. Please note that the graph values are averages and that numbers will vary from place to place due to climate.

Seattle, Washington

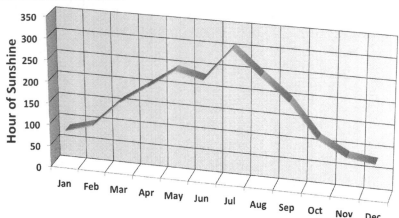

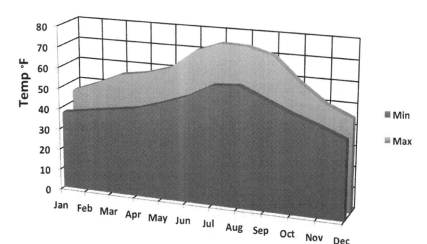

Taking the number of garage sales per week, factoring for the given population and cross-multiplying the square miles, while using the GS scale of zero to 14, the graph on the next page displays the results. Note the similarities in graph curvature. This shows a high correlation between air temperature and the number of garage sales at any given month.

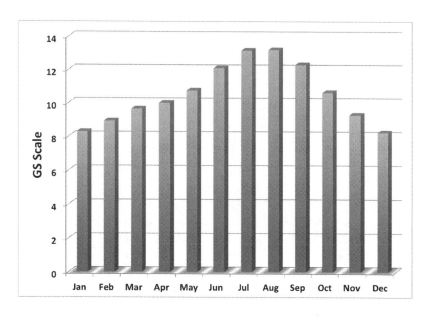

## Pie Chart

And of course, no statistical analysis would be complete without a pie chart. And no statistical analyst would be complete without a slice of pie!

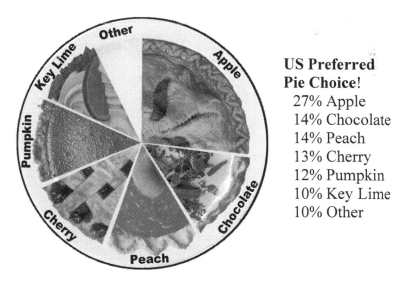

**US Preferred Pie Choice!**
27% Apple
14% Chocolate
14% Peach
13% Cherry
12% Pumpkin
10% Key Lime
10% Other

After having conducted elaborate calculations, I have made an amazing discovery. I have derived the once elusive garage-sale (GS) constant! This constant definitely ranks up there with other significant constants, such as pi (3.1419...), exponential growth constant (e = 2.71828...), and Pythagoras's constant (p= $\sqrt{2}$ = 1.41429...), to name a few. Even chocolate has its own constant.

You ask, "It does?! If so, what is chocolate's constant?!"

Answer: It is always good, all the time and anywhere!

What is not constant about chocolate is when I get to eat it. But as long as it is chocolate, it is fine with me.

But as I was saying, we garage salers now have our very own numerical constant: the GS constant. Here are a few great applications for the GS constant. I am sure once I get a scientific research paper published, others will find all sorts of other applications for the GS constant.

The following photo is a peek at some of my calculations so you can see how I derived the garage sale constant.

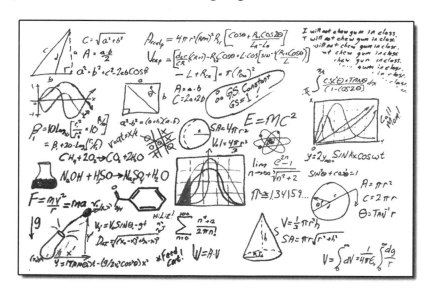

From all this, I was able to derive some initial equations, as shown on the next page.

$$\sqrt{3364}$$

## GS Fun Factor Equation

This equation calculates the amount of potential fun you can expect to have when going garage saling. The more friends you bring, the more fun you have. This equation also takes into account the fun saturation point and declination. At some point, if you invite too many friends along, the fun begins to drop-off. So keep it to a few.

$$\text{Potential Fun} = GS \; \frac{e^{(n^2)/2}}{\sqrt{2\pi}}$$

n = you + the number of friends going garage saling
GS = 1

## GS Fun Summation Factorial

This equation calculates that amount of potential fun one can have in relation to the number of garage sales in your area at any given moment. The more garage sales there are, the more potential fun, which grows by n factorial!

$$\sum_{n=0}^{n} \left( \frac{\tan \emptyset \; \cos\emptyset \; GS \; n!}{\sin\emptyset} \right)$$

n = the number of garage sales in your area
∅ = the present temperature in degrees Celsius
GS = 1

There seems to be a direct relative relationship between the number of people participating in garage sales in a given week and the average temperature for that week. Apparently, the increase in garage sales is directly dependent upon warm air. Warm air is caused by the air molecules becoming more thermally active due to heat or increased thermal inertia.

Therefore, since people are dependent upon air to live, they become more active due to the heated air. Thus, the more active the air, the more active people are. Now, what this has

to do with garage sales, I have yet to figure out. Hey, maybe I could qualify for one of those government grants. I will be sure to publish my findings in my next book.

One woman tried to tell me that the increase in the number of garage sales was because people like to get out more as it gets warmer after being cooped-up all winter. But what does she know. I bet she didn't do any research!

# Deals, Deals and More Deals

*"A bargain is something you can't use at a price you can't resist."*

P. Jones (1887-1929)

ou never know what you might come across. You are sure to find gadgets, gimcracks, gizmos, jiggers, whatnots, and what-cha-ma-call-its. Perhaps you will discover a widget, a thingamabob or a thingamajig. Or, you will make use of more generic terms, such as stuff, items, or things. And as for the more avant garde and sophisticated type, they prefer to refer to such things as objet d'arts, bric-a-bracs, knickknacks, or trinkets.

At some garage sale somewhere, there exists a one of a kind thing-a-ma-jig. They are very rare. That is why most people have not seen one. But if you ever find one at a garage sale, be sure to buy it. It's a keeper. Below, I have included a drawing of a thing-a-ma-jig. If you want, you can go ahead and make one yourself. I tried to patent one of these, but for some reason the patent office kept rejecting my submission papers.

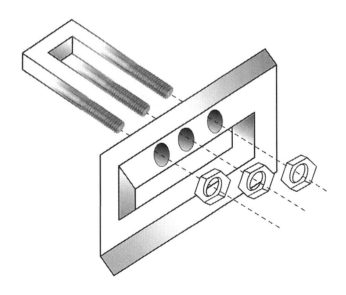

It is always a good idea to be organized. And at garage sales you can often find various storage containers for such purposes. Sometimes, you can find used boxes and even crates that are still in good condition. I was able to acquire a whole bunch of matching crates. They came with hinged lids and latches too. I labeled them and then I came up with a really practical way of stacking them in my storage shed. Below is a picture of my stacking method. I am sharing this with you, hoping that you can make good use of my stacking method as well.

Awhile back I was able to find this very unique item. It was a sawhorse made of pine. As you can see from the picture below, it was in great condition. The seller was unloading it for a great price, so I could not pass it up. The only problem was there was only one of them. I am hoping that sometime soon, I will be able to find another one at a garage sale. That way I can have a matching set. Hey, if you happen to find one, let me know. I am sure I would be interested.

## More Deals

The following are just some of the great deals that you can expect to find at garage sales.

## Tools

Often you can find used tools at garage sales that are in working order. Some tools just need to be oiled and repaired to restore them. Some tools have a lifetime warranty. If you buy one of these at a garage sale, even if they are broken or damaged, it can be replaced for free. This includes such tools as Craftsman and Snap-On tools.

Parts

If you know what you are looking for, you can find replacement parts for lots of things, and at a savings too. Anything from car parts to BBQ igniters. One person may be selling a broken lawnmower at a price that is less than the one part you need to fix yours.

Art Supplies

Garage sales are a great resource for art supplies for crafts and other projects. Sometimes, people are getting rid of all their art supplies before moving onto some other new hobby.

One man scrounged around at enough garage sales and other places to make a portrait of Steve Jobs made out of 5,892 computer keys. It has since been acquired by Ripley's Believe It or Not.

Clothes

Some of the best deals are often clothes purchased at a garage sale. Kids don't seem to ever stop growing, so parents are forever having to buy the next size of something. Some adults seem to be always changing in size too, if you know what I mean.

Here are some great applications for clothes bought at garage sales:

• Baby and children's clothes – Some really great deals on baby and children's clothes as well as toys can be found at garage sales. Baby clothes can be so expensive. But, as you and I know, babies don't stay babies forever and people tend to only have just so many of them. Eventually, they have to do something with all those cute and adorable clothes.

• Dress-up Clothes - Garage sales are also a great place to buy dress-up clothes for your kids. They are inexpensive and therefore you don't have to worry about what happens to them. And often you find some really unique and creative items.

• Craft Clothes - If your kids love to paint, why mess-up some of their good clothes when you can purchase some large shirts and pants that they can wear when painting.

- Rags – You know the words, "Not my good towels!" Many a spousal fight could have been prevented if the husband had only bought some old towels at a garage sale. Some of my best rags have come from old towels. So take my advice men and get yourself some rags today at a garage sale.
- Work Clothes – I know when I garden, I don't want to worry about getting dirty. I just want to focus on gardening. I am the same way whether I am working on the car, welding, painting or doing carpentry. So why ruin your nice clothes when you can find at a garage sale some clothes ready to wear and at a great price, too?!
- Materials for Sewing – I have seen many a creative thing made from old, used-clothes -- jean purses, book covers, patches, quilts, etc. If any of your children are just starting to learn to sew, garage sales are a great resource for materials that are inexpensive and you do not have to worry if they make mistakes or not.

Kitchen Items

Garage sales are a very good place for finding things for your kitchen. If you are not picky about everything having to match, you can furnish quite a bit for your kitchen. Some of the kitchen items you could get at a garage sale can be antiques, if you know what you are looking for. These have an attractive display value. We have some antique cookie cutters hanging on our wall. Sometimes you can buy washboards, mason jars, churns, cast iron meat grinders, and more.

This got me thinking about what it must like to be a spoon. It must be terrible. I would hate to be a spoon. It is not that I hate spoons. Don't get me wrong, they are very useful. I used one the other day to eat my cereal. A spoon can also be used for digging in the garden. Of course I'd use a different spoon. But think about it for a minute. There must be a special place in Heaven for spoons in the afterlife. Think about all the things spoons have to go through! And what about all those places they have go? The next time you go out to eat, take the time to notice all those teeth marks in the dinnerware. Yep, I bet you never noticed them until now. And you thought they

dimmed the lights in those places for atmosphere. Little did
you know that it was to hide all those teeth marks. Just think
of all those mouths that one spoon has been in. Those poor
spoons are going places where no one would dare go again,
unless one was paid to do so, like a dentist or an orthodontist.
All I can say is that I am glad that those spoons at least get a
washing once in awhile. They deserve it. And I am glad that I
am not a spoon.

Just A Few Words About Antiques
    In actuality, antiques are a distinct but yet an intricate part
of the garage sale cycle. They are those items that have been
elevated to a place of high esteem or class and have withstood
the test of time. In so doing, their value has gone up and
therefore they are worth more. Garage sales can often be a
place to find an antique. The general rule that determines if
something is an antique is if it has high value because of
considerable age. To know for sure if something is an antique
takes knowledge and experience. There are several methods
that may be utilized. The one of these ways I have been told is
by measuring the amount of bubble gum that has been stuck
underneath an item. Although this does have some merit, I
have some real problems with this method. First of all, this
tends to be only useful for furniture items. (Whoever puts their
bubble gum under a bowling ball?) And second, it is limited to
furniture that was made after the year bubble gum was
invented. Other than that, it is a fairly sound method.
    But you know what? I know of a restaurant where all the
tables have just got to be antiques. You should see all the
bubble gum! Boy, one of these days, if and when they ever
sell some of those tables, I'm going to buy as many as I can.
Then I will sell them at a higher price to someone else since
they are antiques. So don't you go telling the owner of the
restaurant. This will be our secret.

# Shopping Garage Sales

*"However beautiful the strategy, you should occasionally look at the results."*

Winston Churchill

t garage sales you can find all sorts of things for your home. This is especially good if you have a young family. Most children haven't learned to appreciate quality furniture and glassware like you and I. For them, couches are to be jumped on; any hand-held item is meant to be thrown; dad's shirts make useful rags, etc. So here is a little advice. I recommend that you hold off a few years on buying new things for your home and save money by buying at garage sales. Then, if junior mars, dents, scratches, or breaks (and any other verbs meaning "damages") what you bought, you can say, "No problem. It was just something I bought at a garage sale." This will save you from lots of stress and your kids from any undue wrath. Besides, most garage sale items come pre-dented and broken-in anyway. In addition, this will also provide a way for your children to learn how to begin to respect furniture and other household items without it being at the expense of your china, leather recliner, porcelain lamp, etc.

Besides, you need to live a little. When is the last time you jumped on your couch? You would never consider such a thing if it were new. Think of all the fun you are missing out on. If you got it at a garage sale, there is nothing to worry about.

How much you take into consideration the following information depends upon how serious you are. My advice for a garage sale strategy, is don't take garage saling too seriously. Be sure to enjoy yourself and have fun.

## Time of Year

Believe it or not, garage sales are a year-round event. Most garage sales occur during the warmer months. During the spring, people tend to do their spring cleaning and therefore are getting rid of things. More people move during this time of year as well. This is the peak season for garage saling. The advantage of going during the non-peak season (winter) is that there tends to be less people attending them, so you are more likely to get some good deals.

## Weather

Don't be discouraged by bad weather, even rain or snow. Sometimes days of foul weather can be great opportunities for some fantastic buys. Less people go out in bad weather. This means less competition. And sellers are more likely to sell at a much lower price since so few buyers show up.

## Days

I say any day of the week is a good day to go garage saling. Most garage sales are held on Friday, Saturday and Sunday, with Saturday being the most popular day. Week days are also good days to go. Since most people are at work on the weekdays, there will be fewer buyers at the garage sales. This is why Friday is such a good day to go. We occasionally have garage sales that start on Thursday. I have even seen them on Wednesday.

The best day to go to any garage sale is the first day. By the second day, most of the good stuff has been bought.

## Time

If you are a serious garage saler, then the first few hours of a garage sale are the most important. This allows you to consider items before others do. Therefore, you may want to be one of the first ones to arrive at the garage sale.

In some cases, the last few hours of the sale may also be good for other items. Sellers are much more motivated to unload whatever they have left. This becomes a great opportunity to buy a whole lot of stuff in bulk and for much less.


## Preparation

*"We should remember that good fortune often happens when opportunity meets with preparation."*

Thomas Edison


It is a good idea to be prepared when going garage saling. There is a tremendous wealth of information about how to strategize when going garage saling. And it all depends upon how serious you want to be. What I have done next, is include some of the most important factors to consider. In order to make the most of your experience, do the following:

What to Bring

Cash – Bring change and lots of smaller bills. Try to obtain whatever money you plan on needing at least one day before. Do not take all twenties with you. Be sure to have some quarters, one dollar bills and five dollar bills as well. This allows you to bargain. My experience has been that most people for some reason don't accept foreign money.

Rope, tie-downs and blankets – This is so you can securely transport large and/or delicate treasures home.

Phone – This goes without saying.

Paper and pen – You never know what you may need to write down.

Casual dress – You want to be comfortable when garage saling.

A friend – This makes it more fun! One of you can drive and the other can be a navigator (and keep an eye out for policeman in case you find yourself speeding). The navigator can also keep an eye out for garage sale signs. In addition, you can use your friend as collateral in case you find a deal and are short on cash. That way your friend can stay with the item while you go get some more money. Just be sure to not get distracted by another garage sale and then forget to come back and retrieve your friend.

Snacks and a water bottle – All experienced garage salers know that garage saling can work-up an appetite. Besides, in order to stay on top of your game, you need to keep your energy level up. This also avoids detours to mini-marts when you could be garage saling.

A map – If you are garage saling into unknown or unfamiliar neighborhoods, it is always a good idea to have a map. Fortunately, most phones have some sort of map feature or app. To assist you, I have provided some handy maps in the back of this book. (See **Maps** in back of book.)

Miscellaneous Tips

Be flexible – Anticipate that you may see garage sales that were not on your original list. You might want to check them out.

Check out multi-family sales – Although any garage sale can be an adventure, multi-family ones tend to have more stuff in one location.

Consider going to "inconvenient" garage sales - Ads come in all sorts of ways. Sometimes just by the way an ad is written you can predict that it will lead to a great bargain. For instance, if the ad contains no address but does contain a phone number, chances are there will be less people going to that place. This is because of the inconvenience of having to call to get directions. But this "inconvenience" is to your advantage. That is how I got a great deal on an almost new snow blower.

If the address of a garage sale is in a location that is far away from where people normally travel or is hard to get to, the chances are high that there will be less people attending. Now, if the ad has no address and phone number, you can bet that there were all sorts of good deals. The disappointing part is that no one will know how to get to them.

## How to Prepare

Pick an area – This way you can stay focused and not be
   driving all over the place.

Check the ads – Be sure to check any local papers as well as
   the Internet, as some garage sales will be posted in one
   place but not the other.

Here are some sample attention-getting ads. They have
been condensed and edited to highlight their key points:

---

## Our First Annual Moving Sale - Ever!
## It will be awesome, seriously!

**103 W. 23rd Street, Northtown**

**Get this stuff before we set it up on Sunday!**
(We were going to call this "The Feast on our
Dreams Moving Sale", but that sounded too dire.)
We're going back to school, which means we're
shedding household goods like nobody's business
(except apparently for the lady next door.)! Buy
some outstanding items!
Here are just a few:

**A Rockin' Good stereo system:** As advertised,
it is both rockin' and good. Actual customer
experience may vary.

**K2 Rollerblades with no brakes:** Size 12!
Slightly used! (Is that gross?! Probably. But imagine
the savings!) Non-warty former user.

**A Ladder:** Good for reducing how low to the
ground you are at any given moment.

**"Doodle Pix" Game:** It can be yours for ten
cents. Apparently, we had this game all along. We
are now attempting to correct this situation.

**Brown Aldo shoes:** Didn't fit. (Whoops.) Never
worn outside the house --- size 11 or 12.

**And more!!!**

---

> ## They call it "Eviction" but we prefer "Moving Really Fast" Sale!
> **Saturday 10AM-3PM.**
> 2033 1st Ave., Sunny Springs
> Everything must go! Multiple person/squatter moving sale. Let's face it folks, if you can't make it between 10 and 3 on Saturday, just come by at sundown because all this stuff will be in our trash cans - the blue ones. For pictures of the items, just close your eyes and imagine... Admission FREE, and FREE PARKING!
>
> PS: Come and pet my dog for free. Her breath stinks but she is super sweet.

For more tips concerning garage saling, search the Internet. There are many web sites and blogs that provide a wealth of free information.

Lastly, here are some great, garage-sale-going ideas:

Family tradition – Make it something you do together as a family. It makes it a fun activity to remember and there is always something for everyone, no matter what age.

Nostalgia – You will see things that will bring back memories. And with memories, come stories that start with, "When I was a kid..."

History lesson – How many times have you been to a garage sale and the question was asked, "What is that?" Inevitably someone at the garage sale knows and it becomes a great opportunity to learn something new and interesting.

$$2^3 \; x \; 3^2$$

Fun date – What better way to spend time with someone with similar interests. And what better way to learn about one another's interests than seeing each other's likes and dislikes.

Who knows, perhaps you will meet that special someone at a garage sale - and what better place!

# Bargain Strategies

*"Inequality of knowledge is the key to a sale."*

Deil O. Gustafson

etting a bargain is always fun. Getting a bargain via bargaining can be fun too. But keep in mind that since most garage sale items are already set at bargain prices, there is no real need to bargain for everything. Make it a win-win situation.

So don't be shy; give it a try. If people do not want to bargain, they will let you know and that is fine.

## Be Friendly

Greet the seller with a "Hello" and a smile, while being sincere. People are more likely to reciprocate in kind, and to consider any offers you may give.

## Have a Purchase Limit

Only pay as much as you are willing to spend. This is always a good standard to keep for yourself otherwise you may end up regretting your purchase. Those of you who are more susceptible to garage sale mania have to work especially hard on this one.

## Honor the Seller

Keep in mind that some sellers are expecting haggling while others are not. Be respectful and honor the sellers for their limits. If they do not want to haggle, be nice to them and either pay their price or say, "Thank you" and move on. Giving the seller a hard time because they do not want to haggle is bad garage sale etiquette. Getting a bargain is not about arguing but about negotiating.

## Make Reasonable Offers

Offer less than you are willing to pay, while at the same time, do not offer too little, otherwise this is insulting. This way, if you are counter offered, you might get the price you wanted.

## Combine Items

Offer to buy two or more items at a price less than the combined price. For example, if you see a box that has four things you would like to buy but has some items you really don't want, go ahead and make an offer for the whole box at a reduced amount than if you had purchased the four things. Remember that people want to get rid of things, so by purchasing the whole box or lots of items, you are helping them.

## Honor Your Gut Feeling

If you have negotiated a price and something still does not feel right about it, you do not have to buy it, even if it is a great price.

## Be Willing to Walk Away

Stick to your limits. Tell yourself, "I do not have to buy this." There is nothing enjoyable about having bought something for more than you had really wanted to pay for it. But if it is something very dear to you, then it may be well worth it.

## End-of-the-Day Offer

Make a reduced offer on "end-of-the-day" items. Sometimes people are almost willing to give things away at the end of the day. This is one of the advantages of going late to a garage sale. Sure, you might end-up with some items you don't want. But you will end up with items you did want, and at a much reduced price than if you had done otherwise. The advantage for the seller is that now they don't have to figure out what to do with all

75

the stuff that is left over at the end of the garage sale.

Celebrate

After your day of going to garage sales, be sure to set aside some time so you can go celebrate your day of treasure hunting. Have a mid-day lunch date with your garage sale comrade and share about your bargains.

Questionable Items to Avoid Purchasing

When it comes to getting bargains, there are some things to avoid. I do suggest that you avoid purchasing questionable items even if they do seem like such a great bargain. They will often include low pricing, enticing packaging and wondrous wording to draw you in. I encourage you to resist. To save you from great disappointment, I have made a list of some such items to avoid (although these do make wonderful white elephant or gag gifts):

- Bottled dehydrated water – 100% pure, no additives. Makes one gallon. Just add 1 gallon of water and stir.
- Navy-surplus submarine screen doors. Good up to depths of 20,000 leagues, can withstand sea breezes up to 200 knots. Submarine not included
- Left-handed screwdrivers. Comes with a left-handed hammer for free!
- Demagnetized watermelons (Personally, I prefer my watermelons magnetized.)
- Talking birds (Unless you know the full extent of their vocabulary)
- Unicycle kickstands: reinforced steel, spring loaded
- Refurbished dental floss (even if it has been used only once)
- Reprocessed tissues – half-price!
- Recycled kitty litter – 2 for one sale
- Half jars of mixed nuts (By the way, you never know if those nuts had a previous life as chocolate covered -- I would not take my chances.)
- "Property of the US Government" (or any other governmental agency)

- Parachute: Only used once, never opened, small reddish discoloration
- Fruitcake – (Do you really know where those nuts in the fruitcake come from?)

# Did Someone Say "Fruitcake"?!

*"The worst gift is a fruitcake. There is only one fruitcake in the entire world, and people keep sending it to each other."*
Johnny Carson

on't buy fruitcake at a garage sale?! Why not? You may wonder why I mention such a thing. Well, let me give you the truth about fruitcake, the stuff that no one tells you. You may not like what you hear but this is something you need to know. And if you have gotten this far in the book, you know just how credible my information is.

As tradition would have it, every Christmas there are those who send fruitcakes to their friends and loved ones. Perhaps you are one of these people, either on the receiving or sending end, or both. But little do most know what is really going on. What I discovered has been a long hidden secret of many families. Nobody cares to admit it, but what I am about to inform you of may cause a lot of unspoken family issues to surface. It may even explain and confirm some of the things that you have always suspected but did not want to believe (or, you were too scared to ask). If you feel this might be too much for you, I suggest you skip the following paragraphs and continue on, starting at the next chapter.

Continuing....

Every family has had floating around at least one of what I call "The Family Fruitcake". You know that fruitcake you got from your Aunt Brenda that looks so much like the fruitcake that you thought you sent three years ago to Uncle Bob? Well, you are probably right. It is probably that same fruitcake.

It seems to be some sort of long-lived tradition to pass the fruit cake on to some unsuspecting relative. But just like the dog you left behind when you moved, someday, somehow, it always makes it's way back home. Why, I'll bet that some fruitcakes have been in certain families for hundreds of years. They probably have done more traveling than many of us have ever done in our entire lives. Most people would not dare put a date on them, lest someone someday realizes how old they really are. And I would be wary of those fruitcakes that do have dates on them, since you never know if the date is authentic or not. (The date could have been changed.) Why do you suppose they put so much sugar and sometimes rum in them? And you thought it was to make them taste good.

Nobody would dare to eat the thing. It's petrified. Think about it. Have you ever seen an ant come near one? The dog won't even take a second sniff of it. Oh, he might bury it all right, but you won't see him digging it up again.

The actual reason they put so much sugar in fruitcakes is to preserve them for that long journey ahead. Because it is going to be passed from Christmas to Christmas, they want to make sure they are built for the long haul. Who knows, it may have come over on the Mayflower or when your ancestors immigrated to America. (It is too bad it wasn't confiscated during immigration or tossed overboard. It was probably needed for ballast.)

I think fruitcakes were invented before the practice of design obsolescence. Fruitcakes don't break down. It makes you wonder how fruitcake factories stay in business. My theory is that there are those certain people in the family fruitcake chain who do strange things. You know the type-- they break the link in chain letters. These are the non-traditionalist type. Some say that they actually **eat** the fruitcake. I find this hard to swallow (if you know what I mean). I suspect that they either bury it in the basement or backyard. It makes me wonder how many fruitcakes are in the landfill.

I'll bet there's a lot of trash collectors out there who could tell us some pretty interesting facts about people, just by what they see them throw away. Incidentally, fruitcakes won't rot. Just you wait and see. Someday, archaeologists will be excavating in ancient backyards and discover piles of buried fruitcake. And they will be thankful to me for my information on the subject, bringing understanding as to why and how all these fruitcakes got there in the first place. I would not be surprised if one of those archaeologists took one of those fruitcakes home, dusted it off, washed it, wrapped it up and sent it off to one of his relatives. Nobody would ever know the difference. You have to admit; those fruitcakes are quite incredible.

Every so often, a family fruitcake goes out of circulation, mistaken for a brick, gets misplaced, thrown away, or becomes part of someone's collection. (You laugh, but there are those who collect fruitcakes.) Sometimes a curious person breaks the seal and opens the wrapper. Once you open the wrapper, you might as well throw it away, since the next person will suspect it was passed on. Or, someone foolishly lets their pride get the best of them and doesn't back down on an eat-the-fruitcake dare. As for me, I have learned that you have to draw a line somewhere. I wouldn't do it.

What I have to share next is some wisdom about how to "pass on the fruitcake" while avoiding suspicion. If you receive a fruitcake wrapped in wrapping paper, be careful to not leave any evidence of it having been previously wrapped. Also, it is important to avoid opening the fruitcake tin or foil. This leaves it looking unused. In addition, upon receiving a fruitcake in person, it is always good to say something polite like, "Oh my, a Christmas fruitcake. I would have never guessed!" Or, "You know, a person can't have too many of these."

Some day, the government will probably recall all family fruitcakes. They will then analyze each one's contents while conducting some sort of carbon dating test to verify each one's age. When they publish their findings, you will see that I was right about fruitcakes. It was probably the government who got fruitcakes started in the first place.

By the way, rumor has it that the government has found a unique application for fruitcakes. Due to fruitcake's density being approximately that of lead, it has been found that it works great in shielding radioactive materials such as uranium and plutonium. So now it can be put to a great use, such as in nuclear power plants and doctors' offices for x-ray machines.

The secret is out.  Don't tell me that you have never been part of passing the family-fruitcake around.  Some of you aren't being honest out there.

But if you are one of those who, despite all my warnings, insists on eating fruitcake, then fine.  The least I can do is provide a recipe for some delicious fruitcake for those of you who are avid fruitcake lovers.  This is one that will actually not meet governmental density standards for shielding radioactive materials.  You can find it in the back of the book under "Recipes".  And then you can make it fresh and never have to wonder.  Because at a garage sale, you never know. . .

# A Garage Sale Essential

*"Planning is bringing the future into the present so that you can do something about it now."*

Alan Lakein

I have a significant word of wisdom to pass on to all my fellow garage salers. This piece of advice will save you many frustrating moments and missed opportunities. It is so essential, that I have dedicated this entire chapter to it.

Whether you are a seasoned garage saler or not, you are not immune to what I am about to share. It affects individuals of all ages, races and political affiliations. Even strong men are no match for it. It has brought children to tears and mothers to great frustration. It is one of the great distractions that has ruined many a great garage sale day.

Numerous bargains have slipped past those who failed to apply the following advice. And yet, it all could have been avoided. Strangely, I have yet to find anyone who has listed this among the essentials of effective garage saling.

There is nothing worse than being at a garage sale when it happens, this certain something. It now has taken a hold of you and there is nothing you can do about it. You can resist and ignore it all you want, but it won't make any difference. It only gets worse. And if you don't do something soon, you will have a disaster on your hands. Things can quickly move from annoying to frustrating to embarrassing. So in order to avoid this all together, here is my advice:

Use the restroom before you go garage saling!

And like the first consideration, the second is:
Be sure that all those who come with you do so as well.

Profound isn't it! Boy, do I wish someone had told me this the first time I went garage saling!

# Having a Garage Sale

*"One man's junk is another man's treasure."*

Unknown

elieve it or not, what you consider junk, unwanted or no longer useful, is a treasure waiting for another person to find. Therefore, by having a garage sale, you are creating a treasure hunt for someone else. You are making someone's day. You are bringing potential joy to another's life. You are doing yourself a favor and someone else as well. And people will pay you to take away all your unwanted stuff!

While going garage saling can be done spontaneously, having a successful garage sale cannot. So it is always best to prepare at least one week in advance. For some, I suggest starting weeks in advance, especially if you have lots of stuff. Begin by sorting through all your belongings, setting aside those items that you no longer use or need. Never assume that something you consider worthless would be something no one else would want. You would be surprised! Someone may see an item that is broken as fixable. Another individual may be missing part of a set of something and you happen to have the one item they need. When it comes to garage sales, usefulness is in the eye of the beholder.

## Days

The best days to have a garage sale are when the weather is nice. These days would most likely be during spring and summer. This is when the most number of people will be out garage saling. And of course, Saturdays, Sundays and three-day weekends are great as well.

## Times

Starting in the morning is best. People like to start their day by going garage saling. Keep in mind that sometimes there will be those "early birds" who will come early no matter what time you post.

## What to Sell

Sell anything and everything you don't want anymore. Believe it or not, if it is broken, incomplete, rusty, in disrepair, or even taken apart, somebody may still want it. Besides, it is better to have tried to sell something and to have sold it, than to have thrown it away. There are some exceptions. While some might want your half-full can of old nails, they won't want your half-full jar of pickled eggs.

## Preparation

Set-up – It is best to set-up the night before, having everything organized and ready to be put-out and displayed the next day.

Quantity matters - Have lots of items (60+), otherwise people don't tend to stop. If not, team-up with a neighbor.

Cash - Have plenty of change and lots of ones.

Items on hand:

- Pen and Paper
- Phone
- Tape Measure – handy for customers who may need to measure something you are selling.

Signage – Use plenty of signs throughout your neighborhood as well as one in front of your house. (More on signage later.)

Advertise – Put an ad in the local paper. There are also many web sites that allow posting of garage sales at no charge.

Organize - Group items by category, for example: tools, clothes, books, toys, etc. Have everything ready to be put out on tables, noting where they should go. Make sure that kitchen items are clean.

Arrange clothes - Any clothes being sold should be washed and folded or hung-up for easy access. Do not put clothes in a box to be dug though.

Visibility - Place more desirable items where they are visible so that they can be seen from a car, if possible. Spread things out. The bigger the sale looks, the more likely it will attract customers.

Attraction - Use balloons, banners and streamers – make yours standout. While making it attractive, be sure to minimize any distractions, such as barking dogs and attention seeking pets.

Be creative - A friend of mine went to a garage sale where, as people viewed the items, three young ladies played stringed instruments. Refreshments were also provided. She said that it made her want to linger awhile.

## Take Care of Yourself

- Go to bed early the night before.
- Have a place to sit out of the sun.
- Make a pitcher of iced tea and have it on hand.
- Have snacks and lunch already prepared.

## Get Your Family and Friends Involved

Get your family and friends involved when having a garage sale. I encourage you not to have a garage sale alone. Friends can run errands, get more cash, keep an eye on the merchandise and help answer questions. This is especially true if you get swamped by a lot of people. Also, having company allows you to take turns selling in case you need to (and you will) use the restroom.

In addition, your friends may have things they want to sell. In so doing, this will make your garage sale look larger, which is more attractive to garage sale goers.

Lastly, by having others involved, it makes your garage sale look busier. And people passing by will want to know what is attracting so many people.

## Garage Sale Signs

Garage sale signs are a very important factor. If you don't have signs, you might as well call the whole thing off. Make lots of signs. You should have at least two large signs for your front yard and then a bunch of smaller ones to direct people to your house.

The art of having a good sign is so important. This is something I undertook to research myself, to discover what the ideal garage sale sign would be. (No government funding on this one.) After driving around my town one Saturday, this is what I concluded:

**Sign Size**: No smaller than 2 x 1 feet, but preferably larger. Remember, this has to be seen from a distance and most likely from a moving car. Use sturdy cardboard, not a sheet of paper. You can use paper that is mounted on a piece of cardboard.

**Letter Size:** The words on the first line should be at least four or more inches tall and bold. Print using capital letters; do not use cursive. Letters that are too small are conducive to car accidents since drivers may have to squint as they drive by in order to read the sign.

**Color**: A white sign with black lettering is sufficient. Florescent colored cardboard with black lettering is nice, too. Ideally, all your signs should be the same color.

**Wording**: Brief, brief, brief. This is referring to the amount of words you use, not to what you are selling.

> First line: "GARAGE SALE" in all capitals.
> 2nd line: day and time.
> 3rd line: street number and name
> Last line: an arrow.

This is the minimum. You may want to add an incentive line such as "Everything must go!", "4 Family Sale!", "2 for 1 Sale", "Free Lunch", "Ice-cold, mouth-watering, thirst-quenching lemonade!", etc., as long as it is true, of course.

**City Ordinances**: Know your city's ordinances. Most cities forbid the posting of signs on telephone poles. While some cities have no restrictions, other cites only allow 2 to 3 garage sales per year per household.

**Placement**: Be sure to place signs on the corners of key busy streets. And then have signs on each subsequent street corner, directing people to your house. One way to display a sign is to post it on a stick so that it can be driven into the ground. Another idea is to put a sign on the side of a large box (like a 3 foot tall box), put some rocks, a brick or dirt in the bottom and then place it on a street corner. The weight keeps the box from blowing away. In addition, a box enables you to put a sign on each side in order to get the attention of traffic from all directions. You may want to put the signs out two or more days before your sale so that people know about it. Always go back and remove all your signs after the garage sale. (See example signs.)

Here are some attention-getting phrases to consider putting on your sign or in your ad:

- Everything must go!
- Early birds welcome.
- 60 years of stuff!
- Rain or shine.

- Don't miss out!
- Your treasure awaits.
- Great stuff!
- My stuff needs a new home.

Here are some phrases you may want to avoid using on your garage sale sings:

- Beware of vicious dogs when coming up the driveway.
- Free stuff for sale.

Lemonade Anyone?!

Another idea is to have your kids set  up a lemonade stand. If it is a cold day, have a hot chocolate and coffee stand. They could even sell baked goods and hot dogs. (By the way, it has been noted that if you give away free peanuts, the lemonade sales tend to go up.) Some very committed garage sale goers tend to skip breakfast so they can be the first to those great bargains. They sometimes even push themselves past lunch so that they don't miss out on other garage sales around the next corner. By having refreshments and food items, you are not only doing them a great service, but your kids will be able to make a little profit as well.

If you are lacking ideas of what to serve at a garage sale, check out some of my very own recipes. In the back of the book you will find recipes for lemonade, chili, chocolate chip cookies and, of course, fruitcake.

What to Do with Leftover Garage Sale Items

As with most garage sales, you will have some items that will not sell. These are actually treasures whose intrinsic value your customers failed to see. You have several choices for what to do with the items left over:

1. Store them away for the next year's garage sale.
2. Pass them off to a neighbor who is having a garage sale. (When he's looking the other way, busy with a customer or on the phone, simply slip your box of stuff in amongst all his other stuff. Most people won't even notice.)
3. Keep everything and pass it on to your children. If your children keep up this tradition, then someday these items will become antiques and will really be worth something.
4. Donate them to your local thrift store. Be sure to make a list of what you donate and get a receipt for your records. Such donations are tax deductible.

# Selling Strategies

*"A satisfied customer is the best business strategy of all."*
Michael LeBoeuf

*"To sell something, tell a woman it's a bargain;*
*tell a man it's deductible."*
Earl Wilson

The goal of having a garage sale is to get rid of your stuff, and yes, to make a profit too. So, flexibility is a big part of having a garage sale.

Here are some suggested selling strategies:

- Offer deals. People are looking for deals, so offer deals.
- Consider all offers. If you are not ready to accept an offer, ask them to come back later. Be sure to let them know that if the item hasn't sold by then, you will sell it to them.
- Stick with initial prices for the first few hours even if someone makes a lower offer. Remember, people will be arriving all morning, so you can afford to let a few offers go since others will be coming. Some people even return later.
- Expect to haggle. Some people are expecting to haggle for a lower price. Don't be offended by this. This is part of the enjoyment for them. So price accordingly.
- Drop your prices around noon time and be willing to take offers. Any offer is better than no offer. Remember, you are trying to get rid of all your unwanted items.
- Sell items together at a lower price than if sold individually.

- Take full payment only. If someone says that they will pay you so much now and the rest later but they want to take the item with them, do not do it. You might not see that person again.
- Avoid holding an item for someone who says that they will return with some money unless you give them some sort of deadline. A deadline of an half an hour to an hour to be back is good. This motivates the buyer to return soon. This also prevents you from having to hold an item all day that you could have sold.

Family Involvement

Get your whole family involved but be sure to exercise some supervision. Little Johnny might think he got a great deal when he sold his remote control airplane for 50¢, which you bought him last Christmas. Worse yet, he might have sold your new cordless drill for 75¢. You've got to admit, it was a great deal. (Definitely for the guy who bought it!) Having a garage sale is a good time to teach your children a little about economics and the free enterprise system. Here's a little procedure to follow:

- Have your kids gather up some of their old things that they no longer want. Be sure to check through all their items.
- Assist them in pricing each item.
- Set them up with their own table.
- Let them keep whatever profits they make. Allow them to spend some of what they make towards something they have been wanting to purchase, but be sure to encourage them to put some of it in savings.

The following are some suggestions of things **not** to do while having a garage sale. **Do not**:

Charge admission. You may think you have some mighty fine stuff, but you will soon discover that charging admission discourages most people from coming. If you do have something that was worth an admission price, it probably shouldn't be at a garage sale.

Forget to turn off the sprinklers. You don't want to have the awful experience of all your stuff and all your buyers getting wet unexpectedly. So be sure to turn any timed sprinklers off.

Sell your dad's tools. For some reason no matter how hard you try to explain it, dad just won't understand or share in your excitement about the fantastic profit you made in selling his tools. It's probably the generation gap thing. At any rate, my suggestion is to avoid selling dad's stuff at all costs.

91°F

# Great Quotations in the History of Garage Sales

*"The garage sale must go on."*

Garage Sale Gus

erhaps you may not have known it, but throughout history there has been many an event that was directly or indirectly related to garage saling. Many of these moments owe their inspiration to this favorite pastime. And through such experiences, many have gained tremendous wisdom to pass on to future garage salers, such as ourselves.

So, to inspire you, I have here a few of the great all-time garage sale related quotations, gleaned from the archives of history and literature. Enjoy!

The Declaration of Independence (original 1$^{st}$ draft)
*". . . Life, liberty and the pursuit of garage sales."*

Note: The drafters of the Declaration of Independence felt that they needed to broaden the phrase "the pursuit of garage sales" in order to encompass many other wonderful and enjoyable pursuits. This explains why it reads as it does today as "the pursuit of happiness," which definitely would include garage sales!

Patrick Henry's wife (1771)
*"Give me garage sales or give me death."*

This later provided the inspiration for a famous quotation later to be spoken by Patrick, himself.

## Will Roger's wife: Betty Blake (1930's)
*"I never went to a garage sale I didn't like."*

Evidently she was an avid garage saler herself.

## One man's...
*"One man's junk is another man's treasure."*

Unknown

Variations...

*"One man's fault is another man's lesson."*

William De Britaine's (1717)

*"One man's oversight is always another's gain."*

Thomas Brown( 1720)

*"...as one man's meat is another man's poison, so one man's rubbish is another man's treasure."*

Hector Urquhart (1860)

## Ancient Chinese Proverbs
*"Man who goes to many garage sales has much good fortune."*

*"Man who sticks foot in mouth gets athletes' tongue."*

## Julius Caesar
*"I came. I saw. I conquered."*

Said when getting some great garage sale bargains.

## Juliet from Shakespeare's Romeo and Juliet
*"Romeo? Romeo? Where art thou Romeo?"*

The answer: He was probably at a garage sale.

<u>William Shakespeare (1610)</u>

*"To be {garage saling} or not to be {garage saling}? That is the question."* (From *Hamlet*, III, i, 56-61)

And of course we all know the answer to that question?! Let's "be" garage saling!

<u>Lana Turner</u>

Speaking of garage saling:

*"A successful man is a man who can make more money than his wife can spend. A successful woman is one who can find such a man."*

<u>Sir Isaac Newton's Three Laws of Garage Sales</u>

- A body tends to stay at rest unless it is acted upon by the realization that there is a garage sale going on.
- F = ma: The desire force (F) to purchase garage sale items is equal to a person's "I-must-have-it" motivation (m) times the approximate value of the item (a).
- For every garage sale, there is an equal and better garage sale just around the corner.

<u>Poor Richard's Almanac</u> (Benjamin Franklin's 1st rendition)

*"A penny saved is a penny earned."*

He was most likely referring to the savings experienced when going garage saling.

*"Early to bed, early to rise, makes a man healthy, wealthy and garage-sale-wise."*

This was an earlier rendition before it was edited to encompass more that just garage sales.) As you probably already know, those who go to bed early get an earlier start to those garage sales and thus get the better deals.

## Poker Playing
*"He's not playing with a full deck."*

Note: This was probably said about a poker player who was not a wise garage saler. Evidently, he had not counted the number of cards in the deck he had purchased at a garage sale.

## GS Star Trek
Theme of the mini-series "GS Star Trek":

*"Garage saling: the final frontier. Such are the voyages of many a garage saler. Their on-going mission: to explore strange new neighborhoods, to seek out new deals and new bargains, to boldly go where many a man has gone before."*

*"If you eliminate the impossible, whatever remains, however improbable, must be the truth. Therefore, the only logical action is to go garage saling."*

Spock of GS Star Trek

## Bargaining Quotations
Here are some great quotations on bargaining, providing advice and wisdom from many a garage saler.

*"Life is the greatest bargain - we get it for nothing."*

Yiddish Proverb

*"A miser and a liar bargain quickly."*

Greek proverb

*"Here's the rule for bargains: 'Do other men, for they would do you.' That's the true business precept."*

Charles Dickens (1812-1870)

*"The bargain that yields mutual satisfaction is the only one that is apt to be repeated."*

B. C. Forbes quotes (1880-1954)

*"No one should drive a hard bargain with an artist."*
Ludwig van Beethoven (1770-1827)

*"My old father used to have a saying: `If you make a bad bargain, hug it all the tighter.'"*
Abraham Lincoln (1809-1865)

*"While money doesn't buy love, it puts you in a great bargaining position."*
Christopher Marlowe (1564-1593)

*"When a man is discontented with himself, it has one advantage - that it puts him into an excellent frame of mind for making a bargain."*
Laurence Sterne (1713-1768)

Murphy's Law
*"Anything you buy this week will go on sale next week."*

By the way, garage sales are immune to Murphy's Law!

# Garage Sale Games

*"We do not stop playing because we grow old, we grow old because we stop playing!"*

Benjamin Franklin

 ne of the ways to introduce others to the wonderful experience of garage saling is to invite them along. And while you're garage saling, you might as well play a game and make it extra fun. For your enjoyment, I have included some one-of-a-kind garage sale activities. In the back of the book I have for you a crossword puzzle, a word search, a Sudoku, a maze, and a stereogram. And yes, they are all garage sale related.

Some other garage-sale activities are garage sale games. As a suggestion, you can play one of these at a birthday party or any celebration. Here are some suggested games:

Garage Sale Scavenger Hunt

Object: Whoever obtains everything on one's garage sale list wins.

Players: There must be at least 2 or more players or teams. It is much more fun when you go in teams.

How to play:
- A list of random items is given to each player or team.
- They are given a certain amount of time to purchase all the items at various garage sales.

- All items must be purchased or traded at garage sales only. Nothing may be bought at a store. Also, nothing can be borrowed from someone or be one's own possession.
- Someone says, "Go!" and the hunt begins!

Suggestions: Make sure that the items on the list are inexpensive. Give each team an allotted budget that they have to stay within.

Variations - All items on the list must:
- Be the same color (for instance, blue).
- Start with a certain letter (like "s").
- Follow a particular theme, such as sports, the 80's or spring.

Finale:
- Give out prizes.
- And what to do with all the stuff obtained via the scavenger hunt? Have a garage sale!

Garage Sale Bigger or Better

This is similar to garage sale scavenger hunt except there is nothing to buy.

Object: Whoever returns within the time allotted with the biggest and best item wins.

Players: There must be at least 2 or more players or teams. It is much more fun when you go in teams.

How to play:
- Each player or team is given a small item to start with, such as a paperclip, a used pencil, a thumbtack or a bobby pin.
- The players are given a certain amount of time in which to play the game.
- The players are instructed that they are to go to as many garage sales as possible within the time allotted. At each garage sale they are to inform the person having the garage sale that they are playing "Bigger or Better" and to

ask that person if they have anything bigger or better that they can trade for what they have.

- Someone says, "Go!" and the game begins!

Variations:

- Instead of starting with one item have 2 to 3 items to be traded for individual items. In this way, the person having the garage sale has more to choose from and you can make more than one trade per garage sale.
- Instead of going for bigger or better, go for "more and more". See if you can trade your one item for multiple items. And then trade those items for even more! You might want to call this version "Multiply Mania".

Finale:

- Give out prizes.
- Donate whatever you end-up with to a local church, recreation hall or community center. By informing those at the garage sales of your intention to donate whatever you end up with, it will tend to increase their desire to play along.

# Epilogue

*"Don't cry because it's over, smile because it happened."*
Dr. Seuss

*"Things turn out best for those who make the best of the way things turn out."*
Jack Buck

It has been said that "all good things must come to an end." And so it is for garage sales. Ah, but only for today! For tomorrow there will be more great opportunities, bargains, new discoveries and wonders to behold.

So, keep on garage saling!

# Endnotes

# References

- Bureau of GS
- GS Almanac (not published yet)
- Personal experience
- A friend of a friend
- A friend of a friend of a friend
- The Internet
- My neighbor's cousin's mother, whose nephew twice-removed has a good friend, who knows somebody
- Bureau for the Promotion of Garage Sale Involvement, R&D Division, The GS Building, 5th Floor, Room 201, 3rd door on the left, right next to the drinking fountain.

# Garage Sale Quiz

*"Garage sale trivia: 12 used bowling balls are sold at garage sales every hour."*

Provided by the US Garage-ological Society
of Guess-omology

Here is a small quiz to test your Garage Sale Mania knowledge!

1. How many times does the phrase "garage sale" appear in this book?
   a) 1 - 199    c) 300 - 499
   b) 200 - 299   d) 500+
2. How many garage sales were there in the state of Iowa on September 31, 2001?
   a) 1 - 199    c) 300 - 499
   b) 200 - 299   d) 500+
3. Do you like garage sales? Yes or No
   If you answered "No" to this question, please try the question again.
4. What is the sound of one hand clapping?
5. What is the name of the little garage sale character found throughout the book?
   a) Rupert        c) Gus
   b) Thomas      d) Ginger
6. What was the name of Thomas Edison's son's sister's mother's husband? _____
7. How many garage sales can a garage saler goer go to if a garage sale goer can go to garage sales?

Answers:
1. D) 500+
2. None. There is no day 31 in September.
3. Yes!
4.
5. C) Gus (alias: Garage Sale Gus)
6. Thomas Edison
7. A garage sale goer can go to as many garage sales as a garage sale goer can go.

# Garage Sale Jokes

If you like a good laugh, here are some garage sale jokes.

**Question:** Why did the chicken cross the road?
**Answer:** To get to the garage sale.

**Question:** Why did the duck cross the road?
**Answer:** To try to beat the chicken to the garage sale.

**Question:** When is a garage sale not a garage sale?
**Answer:** When it is a mirage sale.

**Question:** How many garage salers does it take to change a light bulb?
**Answer:** None. Everyone knows that garage salers don't change light bulbs; they go garage saling.

**Question:** Why did the blonde decide not to go to any garage sales?
**Answer:** Because she thought if she were to go, she might end up buying a garage. And if she did, she didn't know how she would ever get it home.

Refreshments Anyone?!

At a church rummage sale as a means to attract people, free refreshments were served. Two tables were set-up in the back, one with cookies and the other with lemonade. Someone had put a sign on the cookie table which read, "Take only one. God is watching." On the lemonade table someone had posted a sign which read, "Take all the lemonade you like. God is watching the cookies."

## A Knick-Knack

One day a frog went to the bank to see if he could get a loan. After inquiring, he was introduced to Mr. Paddywack who was in charge of new loans. While going over all the paperwork and requirements necessary for obtaining a loan, Mr. Paddywack said, "So, Mr. Frog, what do you have for collateral in order to secure the loan?" In reply, Mr Frog said, "The only thing of value I have is this knick-knack, which I got at a garage sale." Upon examining the knick-knack, Mr. Paddywack said, "I am so sorry, but I don't think that will do." Having overheard Mr. Paddywack's conversation with the frog, Mr. Paddywack's senior advisor said, "That's a knick-knack Paddywack. Give the frog a loan!"

## Twelve Dollar Bills

Did you hear the one about the man who printed up some twelve dollar bills? Hoping to pass them off as real  money, he decided to go to a garage sale. When he approached a man running a garage sale, he asked, "Hey, could you give me some change for a twelve?" At first the man gave him a funny look. But then he said, "Sure! How do you want it? 3 'fours' or 2 'sixes'?"

## I Forgot...

Did you know that there are four advantages to having Alzheimer's?
1) You can hide your own Easter eggs.
2) You can make a new friend every day.
3) You can enjoy buying things at someone else's garage sale that you sold the week before at your own.
4) And . . .? Uh...? I seem to have forgotten the last one. Oh well. If I ever remember it, I will be sure to put it in the next edition.

# Recipes

*"Never eat more than you can lift."*

Miss Piggy

Here are some tasty recipes to consider cooking up to serve at your garage sale. Enjoy!

### Garage Sale Chili

*"Next to music there is nothing that lifts the spirits and strengthens the soul more than a good bowl of chili."*

Harry James (1916-1983)

If you anticipate a chilly garage sale day, consider making a delicious pot of chili to "spice it up"! You can sell it by the bowl, or consider advertising "Free chili!" on your garage sale signs.

You will need a 5 quart crock-pot. If you don't have one, go to a couple garage sales and you will be sure to find one at a great price. If the next garage sale isn't for a couple of days and you can't wait to make my chili, borrow a 5 quart crock-pot from a friend. Be sure to give them some of your chili for allowing you to borrow it.

Ingredients
2 (15 oz) cans pinto beans
1 (27 oz) can kidney beans
3 (14.5) oz cans stewed tomatoes (Mexican style)
2 lb. cooked coarsely ground or chopped meat (Add more, depending upon how much meat you like in your chili.)
    Suggestions: regular or coarse ground beef, chicken, pork, buffalo, duck, venison, elk, beaver, moose, bear, etc. (Even though it has                been said that a dog's mouth is more sterile                than

a human's, I do not recommend using something the dog dragged in.)
1 medium onion - diced and sauteed.
1 green pepper - coarsely chopped
2 garlic cloves - crushed
2 Tbs. chili powder
1 tsp. pepper
1 tsp. cumin
1½ cups dehydrated water (optional)

Instructions

Chop onion coarse or fine, depending upon desire, and sauté in a frying pan. Put in crock-pot. In the same frying pan, cook meat. Put cooked meat in crock-pot. Chop-up stewed tomatoes before adding them to crock-pot. Add all other ingredients. Stir. Cook on low for 8-10 hours or high for 5-6 hours.

In Addition…

Be sure to purchase some bowls, spoons and napkins.

Suggestion: offer cup and bowl size portions at different prices.

**Ice Cold Lemonade**

You have heard it said, "When life gives you lemons, make lemonade." But I say, "When life gives you lemons, go garage saling **and** make lemonade!"

Having a lemonade stand is a great way to get your kids involved when you have a garage sale.

Ingredients
1 cup lemon juice
6½ cups water
1 cup sugar

Instructions
Combine all ingredients until sugar is completely dissolved. Best served when chilled and with ice. Makes 2 quarts.

In Addition…
Be sure to purchase some cups and bags of ice.

## Chocolate Chip Cookies

*"All you need is love.  But a little chocolate now and then doesn't hurt."*
Charles M.  Schulz

*"There is nothing better than a friend, unless it is a friend with chocolate."*
Linda Grayson

*"My therapist told me the way to achieve true inner peace is to finish what I start.  So far today, I have finished 2 bags of M&M's and a chocolate cake.  I feel better already."*
Dave Barry

This recipe is sure to be a winner.  Everyone likes chocolate chip cookies.

Ingredients

2¼ cups flour (or gluten free flour)
1 tsp.  baking soda
1 tsp.  salt
2 sticks butter (1 cup) softened
¾ cup brown sugar
¾ cup granulated sugar
2 large eggs
1 tsp.  vanilla extract
2 cups chocolate chips (12 oz package)

<u>Instructions</u>
Preheat oven to 375° F.

Combine flour, baking soda and salt in a small bowl.

In a large bowl combine butter, sugars, eggs and vanilla.

Gradually stir-in the flour mixture.

Add chocolate chips.

Make 1" balls of dough and place on baking sheet. Make
bigger ones for larger cookies.

Bake for 9 to 11 minutes, or until golden brown.

Let cool on baking sheet for 2 minutes.

Transfer to wire cooling rack.

<u>In Addition...</u>
Be sure to purchase some napkins.

Better yet, put 3 to 4 cookies in individual bags and sell by
the bag.

**Fruitcake**

"Memories can fade but a fruitcake lasts forever."
Incognito Independence Fruitcake Festival Participant

Yes, there are good fruitcakes out there. This recipe is for
those who love fresh and yummy fruitcake. Guaranteed not to
last forever since people will eat this one!

<u>Ingredients</u>

1 1/3 c. candied red cherries, cut in quarters

1 c. candied pineapple, coarsely chopped

1 1/2 c. pitted dates, coarsely snipped

1 tbsp. all-purpose flour (or gluten free flour)

1 lb. coarsely chopped pecans

4 oz. flaked coconut

1 can sweetened condensed milk

Instructions

Preheat oven to 250° F.

Grease and flour pan bottom. Sprinkle with flour; toss to coat well.

Combine cherries, pineapple and dates in very large bowl. Add pecans and coconut and mix well. Add sweetened condensed milk; stir well. Spoon evenly into prepared pan, smoothing top.

Bake for 1 1/2 hours. Cool in pan on rack. Remove from pan. Wrap tightly with plastic wrap. Refrigerate at least 2 days. Cake cuts best when cold. Slice very thin with serrated knife.

In Addition...

If selling by the slice, be sure to have plates, napkins and forks on hand. Or, you can have individual slices in bags ready to go. You could even sell by the cake.

# Maps

Whenever you go garage saling, it is always good to have a map so you can find your way or in case you get lost. Then you will know exactly where you are.

**The Milky Way Galaxy**

**Handy "Wherever You Are, Be There" Map**

While garage saling, if you need to get to Anywhere, just use the map I have provided on the next page. It will show you how to get from Here to There, and Back Again. If you have nothing else to do, you can always go to Somewhere. While one can be in Two Places, I have not figured how to be in Everywhere at the same time. Where to go next? If it is not Outofyourway, you can always go Elsewhere. Personally, I would like to live in The Present but some prefer to live in The Past. And if you ever get lost, you are probably in the Middle of Nowhere.

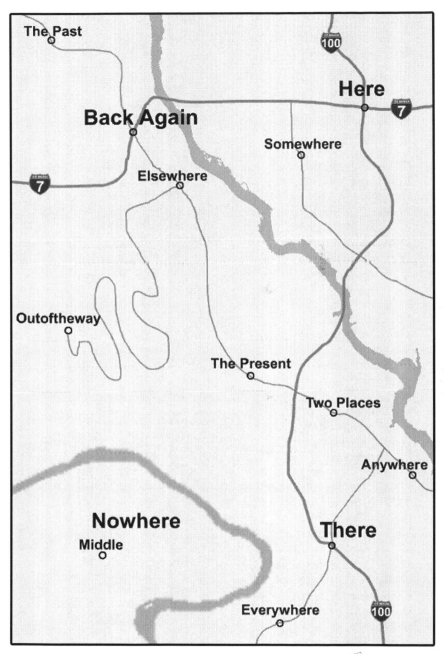

111

# Garage Sale Crossword Puzzle

For those garage sale goers who love crossword puzzles, here is one for you.

## Across

3) Past meet
5) Tri-ski with seat
10) Shows where to go
12) A long search
16) One man's junk
20) Crumbly cheese
22) Hydroxide
23) Small dwelling
24) Candle content
25) Make engine go fast
26) Auctions
28) Many GSers converging
31) GS certified
32) Roman four
33) Short for mother
34) Enjoyment
35) The 6$^{th}$ letter
36) Abv. Laboratory
37) A stiff bristle
39) Precious jewel
43) It's as _____
45) The help of citrus
50) Allows you to hear
51) Perform
52) Resources
55) Ringing sound
57) Another man's treasure
59) Property
61) Handmade items
64) Used to link alternatives
66) Roman nine
68) Used to express agreement
69) Easily fooled
72) Conditional clause
73) Things
74) Not she
75) Refer to a thing
76) Entertaining

77) Task aiding items
80) Canadian last letter
81) Payment leftovers
84) Yes
86) Vietnam money unit
87) A 3-toed sloth
89) Around the house
91) Defective car
92) In the first person
94) Sleeping indicator
96) Major scale: 3$^{rd}$ note
97) Word of mouth
99) An odorized person has this
100) 16 down w/o its thingy, plural
102) Modus operandi
103) A car's room
104) Before the present
105) Philosophy Doctor
106) Prohibit
107) Above
109) A glossy black long-tailed cuckoo
110) Price: men vs. Boys
112) A small worthless object
113) Make reusable
117) Go quickly
118) Facial happy expression
120) Major scale: 6$^{th}$ note
121) Not yes
123) Cubical cardboards
124) Can't hear, say this
126) Internet Protocol
127) A trivial ornament
129) Bird lure
130) Crazy nuts and fruit
131) Weed scratcher
132) Go buy goods
133) Make a request

## Down

1) Thrown overboard items
2) 12th Greek letter
3) Emergency room
4) A rope for towing a boat
6) If and only if
7) Exist
8) Occupational Therapist
9) A good deal
10) In motion
11) A level of equality
13) To stand up
14) To such a great extent
15) Express appreciation
16) Term used when item unknown
17) The chemical element ruthenium
18) Many GSers in one place
19) Best day to go GSing
21) Search unsystematically
29) Items of historical interest
30) Keep for future use
34) Large gathering of small venders
38) Soon parts with his money
41) Mechanical device
42) Abv. This book
46) The jaws or throat of a voracious animal
48) By itself
49) Amusing
53) All the pieces
54) Therefore
56) Matter, material, articles
58) 1,000
60) Informal thingamajig
62) Generic dog name
63) Give in exchange for money
64) Sound: expressing excitement
66) Roman eleven
67) A rigid bar resting on a pivot

71) A non-active volcano in Sicily
77) Beginner or novice
78) GS constant value
79) To go alone
81) A rare, unusual, or intriguing object
82) Sound: short laugh
83) A gadget w/o unknown name
85) Like "down 83" but smaller
88) There is no place like ___
90) Gaseous matter
93) A very excited state
97) What many live for
99) These contain pages
100) Horse's long hair on neck
101) Selling at reduced price, plural
106) Exchange goods w/o money
108) Take delight
114) Contains 52 weeks
115) A monetary unit of Croatia
116) Occur; take place
119) Microphone
120) Go here before you go
122) Slang for yes
123) Not girl
125) Greek: $14^{th}$ letter
128) Used to express surprise
129) Hairdo

113

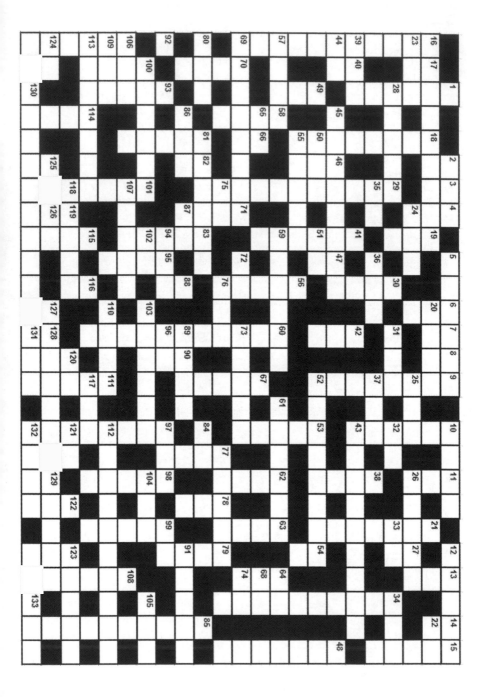

# Garage Sale Mania Sudoku

Fill-in each of the 9x9 grids with the letters in the phrase "Garage Sale Mania", but without using the same letter twice. Thus, only the letters A, E, I, G, L, M, N, R and S can be used. Each row, column and 9x9 square may have only one of each letter in them.

|   |   |   |   |   |   |   |   |   |
|---|---|---|---|---|---|---|---|---|
|   | G |   |   |   |   |   |   |   |
|   | A |   | M |   |   |   |   |   |
|   |   |   | R | S | A | L | E |   |
| G |   |   |   | A |   | N |   |   |
| S | A | L | E |   | G |   | I |   |
|   |   | R |   |   |   | E |   | A |
|   |   | E | A | R | N |   |   |   |
|   |   |   |   | G |   |   |   |   |
|   |   |   |   | L | E | A | R | N |

# Garage Sale Lingo Word Search

- ☐ ANTIQUES
- ☐ ART
- ☐ AUCTION
- ☐ AXE
- ☐ BARGAINS
- ☐ BED
- ☐ BOOKS
- ☐ BOOT
- ☐ BOXES
- ☐ CAMPINGGEAR
- ☐ CDS
- ☐ CHANGE
- ☐ CLOTHES
- ☐ COLLECTABLES
- ☐ CRAFTS
- ☐ DIG
- ☐ DOLL
- ☐ DOOHICKEY
- ☐ ENJOY
- ☐ ESTATESALE
- ☐ FAN
- ☐ FLEAMARKET
- ☐ FUN
- ☐ FURNITURE
- ☐ GADGET
- ☐ GARAGESALE-MANIA
- ☐ GARB
- ☐ GEM
- ☐ GIFTS
- ☐ GIZMO
- ☐ GOODASNEW
- ☐ GSA
- ☐ GSER
- ☐ HATS
- ☐ HOES
- ☐ ITEMS

- ☐ JUNK
- ☐ KNICKKNACK
- ☐ KNIVES
- ☐ LAMPS
- ☐ LEMONADE
- ☐ MAT
- ☐ MEMORABILIA
- ☐ MOVINGSALE
- ☐ MUGS
- ☐ MUSIC
- ☐ PARTS
- ☐ RADIOS
- ☐ RAFTS
- ☐ RAGS
- ☐ RUGS
- ☐ RUMAGESALE
- ☐ SALE (3X)
- ☐ SAVE
- ☐ SAVINGS
- ☐ SAW
- ☐ SELL
- ☐ SHOES
- ☐ STUFF
- ☐ SUN
- ☐ SUPPLIES
- ☐ SWAPMEET
- ☐ TABLES
- ☐ THINGYMABOB
- ☐ TOOLS
- ☐ TOYS
- ☐ TREASURES
- ☐ TVS
- ☐ USED
- ☐ WEEKENDS
- ☐ WHATSYAMA-CALLIT
- ☐ YARDSALE

Just for fun, here are some miscellaneous words to look for:
ALP, ANT, ATE, COAL, DAYS, GO, GRACE, HAUL, HICK, KID,
LEG, LIZZY, MOMS, NEW, NICE, NOT, OX, PING, PIT, SOY,
STATE, TIM, TOE, ZOO (2X)

## Instructions

Test your garage sale eye acuity and see if you have an eye
for seeing garage sale items and lingo, as well as things that
make for a great garage sale experience.

```
S  G  S  E  R  A  D  I  O  S  S  O  Y  M  W  G  R  F
T  S  A  L  V  A  G  E  C  G  I  Z  M  O  H  A  U  L
U  W  V  R  B  E  D  I  U  R  Z  O  B  V  A  D  G  E
F  A  I  F  A  N  N  M  F  I  A  O  O  I  T  G  S  A
F  P  N  T  I  G  M  J  L  T  B  F  O  N  S  E  H  M
C  M  G  F  R  E  E  O  O  A  S  G  T  G  Y  T  O  A
O  E  S  M  G  E  D  S  M  Y  A  R  D  S  A  L  E  R
L  E  I  N  X  E  A  A  A  S  W  A  A  A  M  R  S  K
L  T  A  A  S  D  G  S  J  L  E  C  Y  L  A  U  B  E
E  H  F  U  R  N  I  T  U  R  E  E  S  E  C  M  A  T
C  M  U  S  I  C  R  G  N  R  K  M  G  F  A  A  S  O
T  V  S  H  R  A  G  S  K  C  E  G  A  U  L  G  U  O
A  N  T  I  Q  U  E  S  I  I  N  S  U  N  L  E  P  L
B  O  X  E  S  H  E  H  S  I  D  O  L  L  I  S  P  S
L  T  V  P  T  V  O  M  P  B  S  E  L  L  T  A  L  P
E  A  M  O  I  O  E  M  E  M  O  R  A  B  I  L  I  A
S  A  L  N  D  T  A  U  C  T  I  O  N  I  C  E  E  R
L  C  K  N  I  C  K  K  N  A  C  K  K  T  O  Y  S  T
L  E  M  O  N  A  D  E  G  O  O  D  A  S  N  E  W  S
B  A  R  G  A  I  N  S  E  S  T  A  T  E  S  A  L  E
```

117

# Garage Sale Maze

Help Gus get to the garage sale.

# Flipbook Fun

Ready for some flipbook fun?! There are two flipbook animations contained within this book. Simply flip the pages with your thumb to view them.

**Airplane Banner**

- With the book closed, hold it in your left hand while looking at the back cover.
- Use your right thumb to flip through the pages.
- While flipping the upper left corner, look at the top of the pages.
- It starts on page 2.

**Moonwalk**

- With the book closed, hold it in your right hand while looking at the front cover.
- Use your left thumb to flip through the pages.
- While flipping the lower right corner, look at the bottom of the pages.
- It starts on page 137.

# Stereogram

See what is hidden in the stereogram.

**Instructions:** Bring the stereogram image close to your eyes until it touches your nose. In so doing, your eyes cannot focus on the image and they will look somewhere beyond the image. Now, slowly move the image away while trying to keep your eyes off focus. At some point you will see the hidden image. Be patient and with a little practice you will eventually see the hidden image!

# Stereogram[20] Image: What do you see?!

# Garage Sale Treasure Hunt

Everyone loves a treasure hunt! Scan the cover of the book and find the following garage sale treasures.

- ☐ birdcage
- ☐ keys
- ☐ paddle
- ☐ tie
- ☐ fishing rod
- ☐ unicycle
- ☐ teddy bear
- ☐ floor lamp
- ☐ white dress
- ☐ pink vase
- ☐ toolbox
- ☐ genie lamp
- ☐ motorbike
- ☐ football
- ☐ golf bag
- ☐ gnome
- ☐ milk can
- ☐ Tiffany lamp
- ☐ baseball
- ☐ toaster
- ☐ boxes
- ☐ dartboard
- ☐ oil lamp
- ☐ umbrella
- ☐ lava lamp
- ☐ guitar
- ☐ ladder
- ☐ red wagon
- ☐ couch

- ☐ alarm clock
- ☐ books
- ☐ more books
- ☐ Idaho license plate
- ☐ chair
- ☐ flamingo
- ☐ stroller
- ☐ The Declaration of Independence
- ☐ highway 127 sign
- ☐ rug
- ☐ Uncle Sam poster
- ☐ wheel barrow
- ☐ Mona Lisa
- ☐ top hat
- ☐ old fashioned telephone
- ☐ remote control
- ☐ denim jacket
- ☐ clothes on a rack
- ☐ tricycle
- ☐ American flag
- ☐ Even the kitchen sink!

Bonus!
- ☐ zebra
- ☐ butterfly
- ☐ ladybug
- ☐ grasshopper
- ☐ woodpecker

# Solutions

## Crossword Puzzle Solution

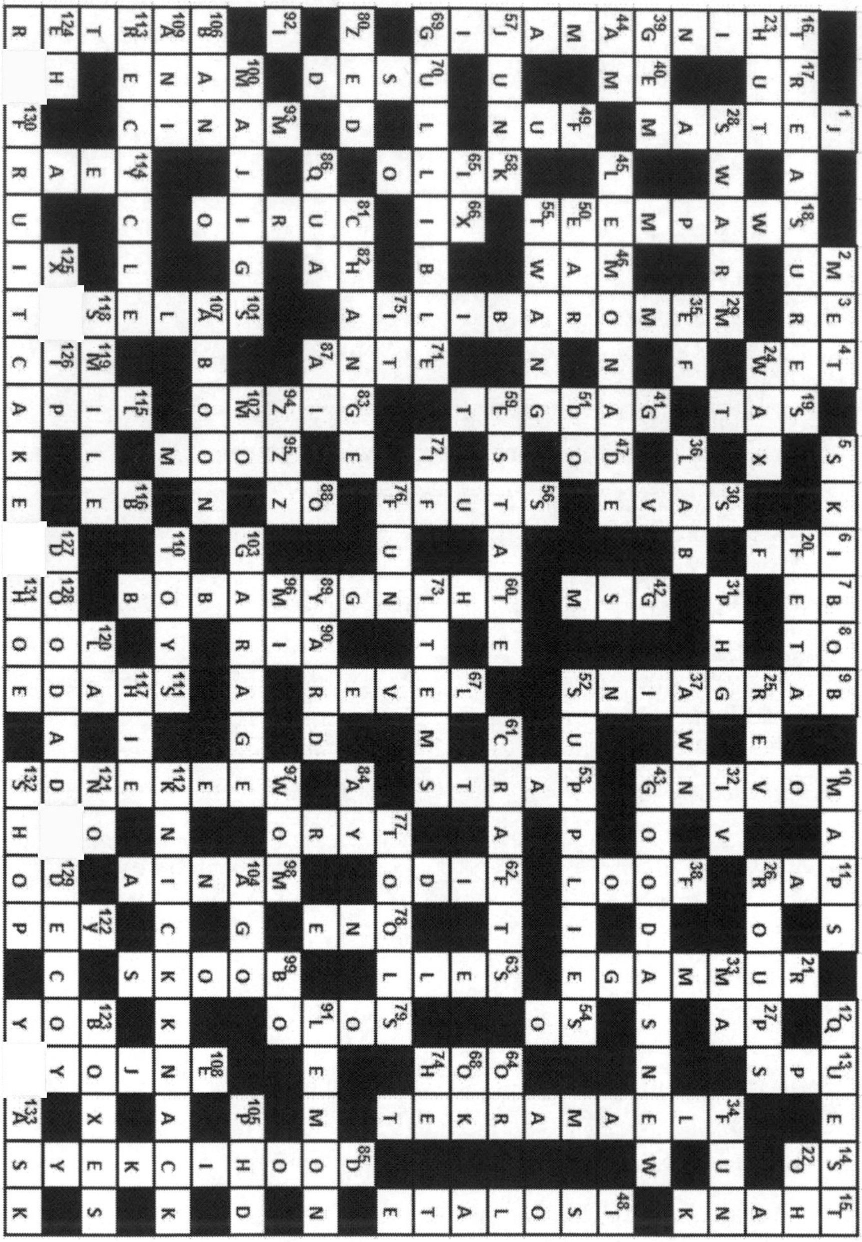

# Word Search and Sudoku Solutions

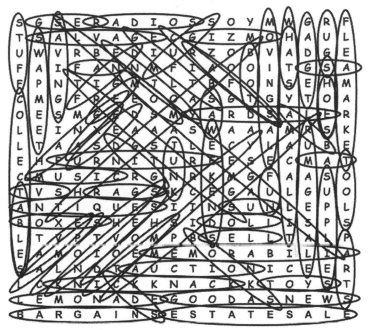

| R | G | S | N | E | L | M | A | I |
|---|---|---|---|---|---|---|---|---|
| E | L | A | G | M | I | S | N | R |
| I | N | M | R | S | A | L | E | G |
| G | E | I | M | A | R | N | S | L |
| S | A | L | E | N | G | R | I | M |
| N | M | R | L | I | S | E | G | A |
| L | I | E | A | R | N | G | M | S |
| A | R | N | S | G | M | I | L | E |
| M | S | G | I | L | E | A | R | N |

## Appendix A - PhG Certificate

PhG: Participant of Humankind in Garage-Sale-ology
   In order to be granted a PhG, just complete the following four easy steps:

1) Attend a garage sale or have one within the next month.

2) Share your experience with a friend.

3) Raise your right-hand and repeat the Official Garage Sale Oath.

*I, (say your name), promise that:*
   *I will introduce others to the wonderful and enjoyable activity of garage saling.*
   *I will practice the activity of garage saling as much as possible.*
   *I will play fair with my fellow garage salers.*
   *I will not purchase anything that is more than I am willing to pay.*
   *I will not use foul language at long stop lights or if caught in slow traffic while attempting to get to a garage sale.*
   *I will not covet the bargains of other fellow garage salers, but promise to "Oo!" and "Ah!" at their finds.*

4) Write your name and date on the certificate.

That's it! It is now official!
You now have your PhG!

# Participate of Humankind

## in

## Garage-Sale-ology

In recognition of outstanding involvement while maintaining the Garage Sale Code, this PhG certificate entitles the bearer to all rights and previledges therein.

Name: _____

Date: _____

*RJ Morrisette*
Prof. of Garage Sale Mania

*Garage Sale Gus*
Garage Sale Gus

## Exhibit A – Garage Sale Bumper Stickers

Spread the word. Here are some sample bumper stickers you might want to add to your bumper.

**Honk if you love going garage saling!**

**Garage Sales: One is not enough!**

**Say, "Go!" to garage sales!**

**My wife was garage saler of the month!**

## WHEN THE GOING GETS ROUGH THE TOUGH GO GARAGE SALING!

## REAL MEN GO GARAGE SALING!

## WARNING: I brake for garage sales!

# Exhibit B - Garage Sale Mania Translations

The following are various translations of the book's title:

**Garage Sale Mania**

| Language | Translation |
|---|---|
| Spanish | Venta de garaje manía |
| French | Vente de garage manie |
| German | Garage Verkauf Manie |
| Italian | Garage vendita mania |
| Irish | Gharáiste mania díol |
| Japanese | ガレージセールマニア |
| Hebrew | מאניה מכירת מוסך |
| Greek | γκαράζ προς πώληση μανία |
| Russian | продажи гаража мания |
| Vulcan | Pi'hali-kel makau tepor'es |
| Klingon | gh 'oH Qanghachpat'e' DIlmeH SeymoH |
| Pig Latin | Aragegay Alesay Ainmay |
| Hawaiian | Hale ka'a Ku'ai aku Hau'oli, 'oli'oli |
| Elmer Fudd | Gawage Sawe May-aynia |
| Swedish Chef | Gerege-a Sele-a Muneea |

## Computer Languages

| | |
|---|---|
| ASCII | 71 97 114 97 103 101 32 83 97 108 101 32 77 97 110 105 97 |
| Hexadecimal | 47 61 72 61 67 65 20 53 61 6C 65 20 4D 61 6E 69 61 |
| Octal | 107 141 162 147 145 040 123 141 154 145 040 115 141 156 151 141 |
| Binary | 01000111 01100001 01110010 01100001 01100111 01100101 00100000 01010011 01100001 01101100 01100101 00100000 01001101 01100001 01101110 01101001 01100001 |

# Index

# Glossary

The following are some very helpful garage sale terms (and other miscellaneous words) that exist within and owe their etymology from the wonderful world of garage saling. This list is by no means exhaustive but it is a good place to start. And I am sure you, too, may have some great "garage sale lingo" that you could add to this list!

## A-C

**antique** - (literally) something of high value because of its considerable age; (gadgetilogically) anything that has become obsolete, such as computers and other electronic devices that are older than 4 years.

**auction** - a competitive, fancy garage sale where items are sold one at a time by bidding and the highest bid wins. These are lots of fun, too.

**balderdash** - two hairless men trying to outrun each other to a garage sale.

**bargain** - something you don't need, at a price you cannot resist.

**bauble** - a small trinket or decoration.

**be going** – to have to leave usually to go somewhere else more important.

**bibelot** - (see tchotchke)

**bric-a-brac** - curious or antique articles of virtu; odd knickknacks.

**cell phone** – a device used by microscopic creatures to communicate over long distances.

**Chargoggagoggmanchauggagoggchaubunagungamaugg** - The name of a lake in Massachusetts.

**credit card** - a monetary device which allows you to put off payment until tomorrow what you bought today, while you are still paying off what you bought yesterday.

**curios** - any article of virtu.

## D-F

**delay** - please check back later for the definition of this word as it is not available yet but will be soon. We apologize for any inconvenience this may have caused.

**dig** - attempting to locate a find among other items.

**doen** - when something is done but perhaps not done right.

**doohickey**
1) unlike a thingamabob but similar.
2) usually some obscure looking but very useful homemade tool that no one knows what it really does but it sure comes in handy.

**doodad**
1) a miscellaneous accessory or trinket.
2) when dad gets his hair done very fancy-like.
3) a dad that does stuff.

**dumpster diving** – the unorthodox, non-Olympic sport of rummaging through dumpsters for unwanted and disposed of items.

**early birds** – garage salers who show bad garage sale etiquette by showing-up at a garage sale before the posted time.

**estate sale** - a garage sale classification where items being sold tend to consist of most but not all the possessions of an owner.

**find** (as in "a find") - a bargain.

**frippery** - (see bibelot)

**flea market**
1) a consolidation of multiple garage sales, like a swap meet but smaller.
2) a regular gathering where people buy and sell new and used siphonapteras.

**floccinaucinihilipilification** - the act of estimating (something) as worthless. This is a great word to use to impress your friends when garage saling upon discovering an item of no value.

# G-I

**gadget** - A "useful" (or so you were told) kitchen or shop item that you bought from a salesman that later ends up being sold at a garage sale.

**gadgetilogical** – having the qualities or traits of a gadget.

**garage-ology** - the study of those things having to do with garage saling.

**garage sailor** - any military personal of the US Navy who enjoys going to garage sales.

**garage sailing** - the non-recommended activity of attempting to maneuver a garage through water using a mast and a sail. Since garages do not float, this does not end well.

**Garage-sale-asize** – a series of videos showing various arobic exercises you can do while going garage saling.

**garage-sale-osmos** - having to do with the garage sale universe seen as a well order, harmonious system.

**garage sale** - like a yard sale, but the items being sold are on display in one's garage and driveway. The terms "garage sale" and "yard sale" tend to be used interchangeably.

**garage saler** - a person who participates in garage sales who can be either the buyer or the seller.

**garage saling** - the act of being involved in garage sales.

**garage seller** - one who sells garages.

**garage sold** - when a garage seller successfully sells a garage.

**gaud** - a showy and purely ornamental thing.

**gawn** - a southern expression for when someone has left or when a baseball is hit out of the ballpark, as in "It's goin', goin', gawn!"

**gewgaw** – a small object displayed for its attractiveness or interest.

**gimcrack** - a cheap and showy ornament; a knickknack.

**gizmo** - a device which one does not know the name for.

**go** - to proceed, to depart. (As in: "Let's go garage saling!")

**goed** - the past tense of go, as in: "went". "Goed" was used before the word "went" was invented. Since then "goed" has lost its popularity and it has become more fashionable to say "went" instead. So goed is gone.

**goee** - the one to whom the goer goes.

**goer-** one who goes.

**goers-** more than one goer.

**goes** - what a goer does best.

**goest** - the old English word for "go" when used with the pronoun he, she, it or they. As when William Shakespeare asked his wife, "Woman, where thou goest?" To which she replied, "I goeth garage saling!"

**goeth** – the equivalent of "you go" when using the word "thou" in a sentence (go see "goest" for more information).

**go-in** – something that is on its way.

**going** -the moment a goer goes and is still in motion.

**go it alone** – to undertake a task or adventure by one self. However, we always recommend going garage saling with a friend.

**gon** – (*gahn*) this is how "gone" is pronounced and should have been spelled. But whoever follows the rules of English anyway?! Or, should "gone" be pronounced "*gun*" as in the word "one"? Or, should it be "goen" as in the word "*lone*"? Funny thing, the English language.

**gone** – (*gahn*)

1) what occurs after a goer goes.

2) what occurs when you hesitate and someone else buys a bargain before you do - It's gone! (Quick, be sure to look at the word "hesitate"!)

**goner** - a goer who came and went.

**gonna** - the action of going to go.

**gown** – a very fancy dress that a woman wears when she goes to a formal occasion, such as a ball, but not appropriate attire for attending a garage sale.

**goze** - (Would you believe that I couldn't find this one in the dictionary?)

**GSA** - short for: garage sale addiction, or for someone who is a "garage sale addict".

**GSAA** - short for: Garage Sale Addicts Anonymous

**GSAC** - short for: Garage Sale Auto Club (Tell them that you heard about them through my book, and they will give you a membership discount!)

**GSM** – short for: Garage Sale Mania

**GSer** - short for: garage saler

**GSing** - short for: garage saling

**GSGJ** - short for the Garage Sale Goer's Journal. A monthly publication dedicated and geared towards the garage sale enthusiast. (Let me know where I can get a copy.)

**GSW** - short for a "garage sale wanna-be".

**GSZ** – (As far as I know, this does not stand for anything.)

**gullible** - easily fooled (This definition was provided since the definition of it does not exist in the dictionary.)

**hesitate** - Sorry, but you waited too long; which is definitely something you do not want to do when you see a bargain at a garage sale.

**humuhumunukunukuapuaa** - a name of a tropical Hawaiian fish rarely seen at garage sales, unless perchance you are lucky enough to see one at a Hawaiian garage sale. The Hawaiian literal meaning is "a fish whose snout looks like a pig."

**IGSA** - the International Garage Sale Association, an international organization committed to the awareness and study of the on-going phenomenon of garage saling.

**irony** - a nonfatal condition that occurs to one's knees whenever one attempts to remove wrinkles from one's pants prior to removing one's pants first.

## J-L

**jigger** - any of various mechanical devices, many of which have a jerky or jolting motion, which are similar to a gadget but more proportional in size.

**junk** - a relative term for items of either great worth or worthlessness, depending upon one's perspective.

**junkie** – an addict.

**kitty litter** - the unlawful practice of discarding small felines along the roadside.

**knick knack or knickknack** - a small treasured trinket

**Llanfairpwllgwyngyllgogerychwyrndrobwllllantysiliogogog och** - (58 letters!) the famous name of a real town in the United Kingdom (possibly known for its garage sales).

## M-O

**majig** - a thingymajig that lost its thingy (see "thingymajig")

**mania** - marked periods of great excitement, euphoria, delusions, and over-activity. Has been known to afflict many a garage saler.

**microwave** – how single celled creatures greet one another.

**MSG** – Garage Sale Mania abbreviated backwards.

**no go** – to cancel, abort; as in "It's a no go."

**non-existent** - (see "zooberfy")

**objet d'art** - an article of artistic worth.

**on the go** – to be energetic and active.

## P-R

**paradox**
1) the dilemma of not knowing where to tie-up one's boat when there are two docks to choose from.
2) when two doctors get married who previously had the same last name.

**passing-the-buck** - (see "refer")

**PhG** – Stands for: Participant of Humankind in Garage-Sale-ology (see Appendix A)

**pneumonoultramicroscopicsilicovolcanokoniosis** - a lung disease caused by the inhalation of very fine silica or quartz dust often suffered by miners. But this is not something you need to worry about when going garage saling.

**postcognitive** – the ability to remember things after they happen; the opposite of precognitive.

**redundant** – redundant.

**redundant** – redundant.

**refer** - (see "passing-the-buck")

**reluctant** - (You may not want to read the next word !)

**repeat**
1) repeat.
2) Note: see definition 1.

**rip-off** - bad garage sale etiquette.

**rubberneck** - a condition of one's neck that often occurs to many a seasoned garage saler.

## S-U

**shin** - a useful device used to find furniture in the dark.

**slibberdits** - a polite word of exclamation most appropriately used when frustrated, as in "Oh slibberdits!"

**spillchecker** - a specialized bib used when eating alphabet soup.

**stuff** - the garage sale lingo for the sum of all the items either to be sold at a garage sale or all the items that one bought during one's day garage saling.

**supercalifragilisticexpialidocious** - amazingly excellent! A most fantabulous word to describe a successful day of garage saling.

**swap meet** - a consortium of garage sales all within the same location. (Not to be confused with the annual butchers exchange convention, as in "swap meat".)

**Taumatawhakatangihangakoauauotamateaturipukakapiki maungahoronukupokaiwhenuakitanatahu** - the actual name of a hill in New Zealand (not necessarily known for its garage sales).

**tchotchke** – (see frippery)

**thrift store** – a great place to find used items at low fixed prices.

**thingamabob** - like a doohickey but different.

**thingymabob** - the gizmo perpendicular to the thingamabob that supports the whatchamacallit, which allows the wizzbang to engage with the doohickey.

**thingamajig** - different than thingamabob but similar (sometimes spelled "thingumajig").

**thingumabob** - used instead of a specific name that one has forgotten or does not know.

**to go** – to order food, as in: take away.

**trinket** - a cherished item, usually small in size.

**unknown** - ???

## V-X

**vagueness** - give me ambiguity or give me something else.

**valutivity** – the property or quality of something having value or worth.

**virtu** - a love of, or taste for, curios or objets d'art.

**wanny** - a person who complains too much. A wanny is someone you definitely would not want to bring garage saling with you.

**whatnot** - a nondescript object or article.

**whatchamacallit** - an all purpose word which expresses, "I know what you mean" without you having to say it. It's an evasive way of saying, "I forgot what it is called."

**whizbang** or **wizzbang** - a gizmo that has a lot of sound, excitement and appeal.

**widget** - a small mechanical device, as a knob or switch, especially one whose name is not known or cannot be recalled.

## Y-Z

**yard sale** - like a garage sale but the items being sold are on display in one's yard. Yard sale and garage sale tend to be used interchangeably.

**ZOWIE!** - after reading this book, this is the word (or one like it) that typically comes to mind as you feel this increased desire to go garage saling. As in: "Zowie! I can't wait to go garage saling!"

**Garage Sale Wish List**

Using the following pages to write-out your garage sale wish list today!

Made in the USA
Lexington, KY
11 October 2015